THE ILLUSTRATED HISTORY OF THE WORLD

The Earliest Civilizations

PREFACE

The Illustrated History of the World is a unique series of eight volumes covering the entire scope of human history, from the days of the nomadic hunters up to the present. Each volume surveys significant events and personages, key political and economic developments, and the critical forces that inspired change, in both institutions and the everyday life of people around the globe.

The books are organized on a spread-by-spread basis, allowing ease of access and depth of coverage on a wide range of fascinating topics and time periods within any one volume. Each spread serves as a kind of mini-essay, in words and pictures, of its subject. The text—cogent, concise and lively—is supplemented by an impressive array of illustrations (original art, full-color photographs, maps, diagrams) and features (glossary, index, time charts, further reading listings). Taking into account the new emphasis on multicultural education, special care has been given to presenting a balanced portrait of world history: the volumes in the series explore all civilizations— whether it's the Mayans in Mexico, the Shoguns in Japan or the Sumerians in the Middle East.

The Earliest Civilizations

Margaret Oliphant

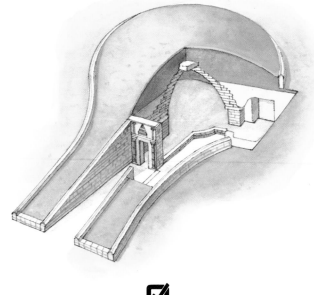

Facts On File

Facts On File, Inc.
460 Park Avenue South
New York NY 10016

Oliphant, Margaret.
The earliest civilizations/Margaret Oliphant.
p.   cm.
Includes bibliographical references and index.
Summary: Explores the history of the world from the time of the early
hunters and farmers to the rise of ancient Greek civilization and the
first empires of China.
ISBN 0-8160-2785-4
1. Civilization, Ancient—Juvenile literature.
[1. Civilization, Ancient.]   I. Title.
CB311.045   1993
930—dc20
91-41428
CIP
AC

ISBN 0 8160 2785 4

Facts On File books are available at special discounts when purchased
in bulk quantities for businesses, associations, institutions or sales
promotions. Please call our Special Sales Department in New York at
212/683-2244 (dial 800/322-8755 except in NY, AK or HI).

Designed by Hammond Hammond
Composition by Goodfellow and Egan Ltd, Cambridge
Printed and Bound by BPCC Hazell Books, Paulton and Aylesbury

10 9 8 7 6 5 4 3 2 1

This book is printed on acid-free paper.

First Published in Great Britain in 1991 by
Simon and Schuster Young Books

CONTENTS

INTRODUCTION

Somebody once called the past 'a foreign country where people do things differently.' This is a helpful way of thinking about the past, for we can all imagine visiting another country and discovering how different it is.

In this book we are going to discover the distant past. Our journey begins millions of years ago when people first existed and ends with the earliest cities and states that were created over 4000 years ago.

The maps will help you to see where things happened and the timecharts will show you when they took place.

But how do we actually know what happened so long ago? Well, knowledge of the past is based on *evidence*, much of which is found by *archaeologists* digging or excavating ancient cites. Non-written evidence such as skeletons of humans or animals, seeds and pollen, fragments of pottery or jewelry, stone or metal tools and weapons or the remains of buildings, are called *material remains*.

For the long period before the invention of writing, which is called *prehistory*, it is from the evidence of material remains that we can reconstruct what probably happened. For example, the fortifications built at Jericho in about 8000 BC show us that the city needed to defend itself, that it was wealthy enough to build such walls, and, because objects from distant places were found here, we can assume that there was extensive trade, which is probably why the city was wealthy.

But, without written evidence, we can know nothing of particular events. With the invention of writing and the keeping of records, the past becomes history filled with real people and the accounts of their actions.

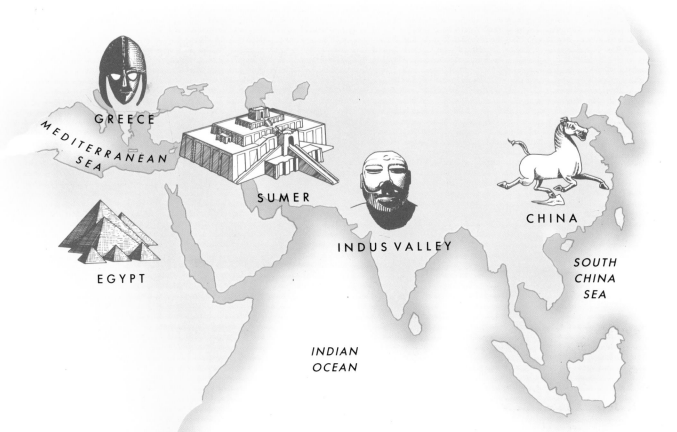

PART ONE

The First People

More than 5 million years ago, scientists believe, our ancestors first came down from the trees and became separated from the apes.

It took several more million years for our species, *homo sapiens sapiens*, to emerge. By then, our ancestors were making tools from pebbles and stones, and using fire.

Since that time, nearly 100,000 years ago, mankind's technological advances have been immense. However, it has only been in the last 10,000 years or so that so many skills that we take for granted have developed – such as the development of farming, metalworking and textile-making.

Whereas for thousands of years people have used ceramic plates and pots, and metal saucepans, nowadays our technology changes so rapidly that it is possible to imagine a very different world. A world in which plastic plates and dishes and microwave ovens replace the need for metal pans and ordinary ovens. Such changes have taken place in decades rather than, as formerly, in centuries.

Until recently – and even now in some countries – people used many tools and techniques little different than some of the inventions of the ancient world.

Part One traces mankind's journey from our beginnings to the first cities and states. In between these two points, there was adaptation and invention as our ancestors evolved from nomadic hunter-gatherers to settler-farmers, and later to city-dwellers.

Stone and, later, metals were worked, and pottery and clothmaking developed. Prehistory ends with the invention of writing and the keeping of written records. From these we can learn something of the history of the earliest civilizations.

HOW MANKIND BEGAN

Man's history is very short compared with the history of the Earth, which scientists think is about 4,550 million years old. If you think of this book as containing the history of our planet, human history would only fill the last three lines of the last page.

Although our existence is so relatively brief, it took several million years for humans to develop. This process, called *human evolution*, was not only lengthy, but was also very complex and is still not fully understood.

THE PRIMATES The closest living relatives of humans are the great apes; both belong to the group of animals called *primates*, which includes monkeys. Humans however, differ from apes in three significant ways: their brains are larger, they walk upright on two feet, and use their hands with great dexterity.

THE SEPARATION OF APES AND HUMANS Once, man and ape had a common ancestor, but some time between eight and five million years ago, the separation of humans from apes took place. In a period of increasing dryness, the forests of Africa receded and the area of grasslands became greater. Apes lived in the trees of the forests and as the numbers of trees decreased, only the strongest apes remained in the forest, while those who were weaker were pushed out.

These weaker apes, who were the ancestors of man, had to adapt to a life in open grasslands. They had to learn to move quickly as they were more exposed and gradually their bodies became adapted to running and walking upright rather than swinging from trees.

Because they were less strong and less protected outside the forest, they learned to use tools to protect themselves and to kill other animals. Their life was more difficult and complex than that of the ape in the forest and they were physically weaker, so their brains developed as they learned more skills. So it was originally because they were physically weaker than the apes that our ancestors adapted and survived.

AUSTRALOPITHECENES From fossil remains we know that creatures called *australopithecenes* (southern apes), lived in Africa between four and 1.7 million years ago. They were 4 feet tall and had small brains, but they walked upright. A female skeleton found in Ethiopia – named Lucy after the Beatles' song 'Lucy in the Sky with Diamonds' – belongs to the earliest type or species of australopithecenes. Dated to 3.4 million years ago, her small body, while partly ape-like, had an upright posture and teeth with human characteristics. Some scholars think that Lucy's species was the ancestor to the earliest type of man. Others think that man, or *homo*, evolved separately. Man's origins are still uncertain and are the subject of much debate.

PREHISTORIC HANDYMEN By about two million years ago, australophithecenes and the earliest species of man, called *homo habilis*, 'handyman,' were living at the Olduvai Gorge in Tanzania. 'Handyman' probably made the first stone tools, called *Olduwan* after the site. These simple tools made by chipping flakes from pebbles, are a landmark in human evolution. They show that homo habilis could plan, because he made special tools for particular tasks. This is something that other animals cannot do.

UPRIGHT MAN *Homo erectus*, 'upright man' was in Africa, China and Java by about 1.5 million years ago. By 700,000 BC Europe had been colonized. These people used fire, hunted large animals and made increasingly specialized tools.

WISE MAN By 120,000 BC early forms of *homo sapiens*, 'wise man,' had emerged. These early stages of human development in the old *Stone Age* are called the *Lower Palaeolithic* period, from the Greek words for 'old' and 'stone.'

Skull Finds of Early Man

Australopithecene   **Homo habilis**   **Homo erectus**   **Homo sapiens**

The remains of the oldest hominids have been discovered in Africa. Olduvai Gorge became especially famous following the first discovery of a skull of the homo habilis type made there by anthropologist, Louis Leakey, and his wife, Dorothy.

The fossil homo habilis could be distinguished by its larger brain, rounded skull and less ape-like face. Developments from the homo habilis skull show a progressive trend towards anatomical features that we can easily recognize as 'human.'

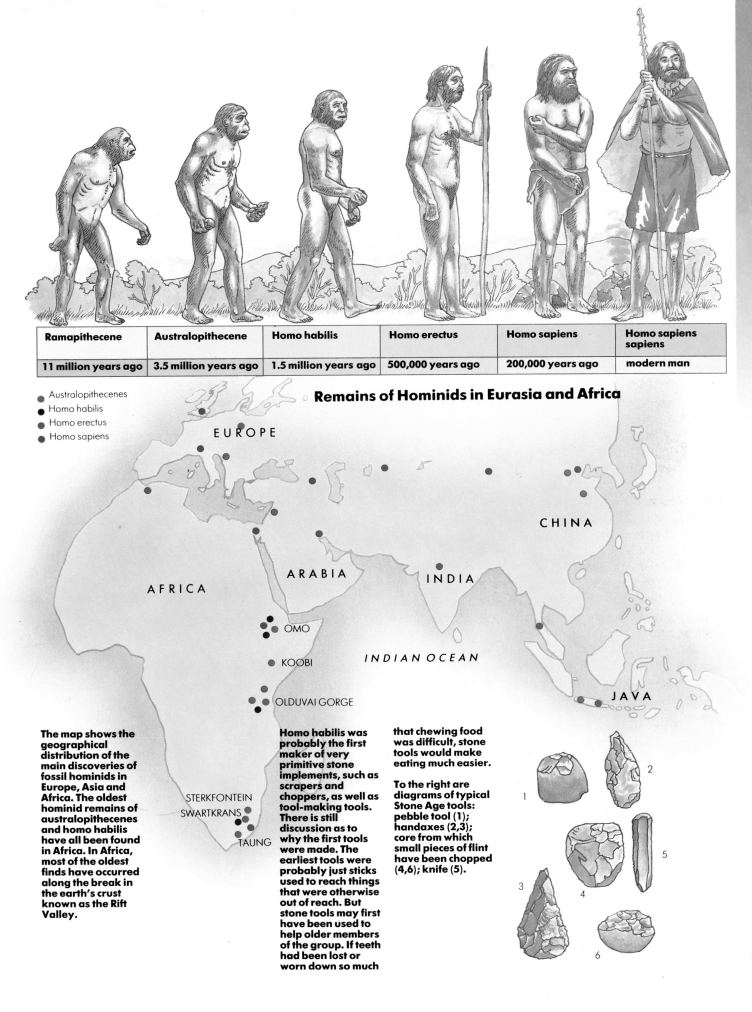

Ramapithecene	Australopithecene	Homo habilis	Homo erectus	Homo sapiens	Homo sapiens sapiens
11 million years ago	3.5 million years ago	1.5 million years ago	500,000 years ago	200,000 years ago	modern man

- Australopithecenes
- Homo habilis
- Homo erectus
- Homo sapiens

Remains of Hominids in Eurasia and Africa

EUROPE

CHINA

AFRICA

ARABIA

INDIA

OMO

KOOBI

INDIAN OCEAN

OLDUVAI GORGE

JAVA

STERKFONTEIN

SWARTKRANS

TAUNG

The map shows the geographical distribution of the main discoveries of fossil hominids in Europe, Asia and Africa. The oldest hominid remains of australopithecenes and homo habilis have all been found in Africa. In Africa, most of the oldest finds have occurred along the break in the earth's crust known as the Rift Valley.

Homo habilis was probably the first maker of very primitive stone implements, such as scrapers and choppers, as well as tool-making tools. There is still discussion as to why the first tools were made. The earliest tools were probably just sticks used to reach things that were otherwise out of reach. But stone tools may first have been used to help older members of the group. If teeth had been lost or worn down so much

that chewing food was difficult, stone tools would make eating much easier.

To the right are diagrams of typical Stone Age tools: pebble tool (1); handaxes (2,3); core from which small pieces of flint have been chopped (4,6); knife (5).

NOMADIC HUNTERS OF THE STONE AGE

During the Lower Paleolithic period there were many changes in climate. The first of the four great *Ice Ages* began about 1.5 million years ago. During this time the weather was much colder, and snow and sheets of ice covered most of Northern Europe.

Because mankind's ancestors could think and plan ahead, they were able to survive the harsh conditions of the Ice Ages. Their tool-making skills developed, they used fire, made clothing and shelter and became more proficient at hunting animals and gathering plants. They lived in small groups as *nomads*, constantly on the move in search of food. Sometimes they would stop at certain places where there were many plants or animals to hunt.

NEANDERTHAL MAN The last Ice Age began about 70,000 BC, and during its early stages Europe and parts of Asia were inhabited by a species called *Neanderthals*. This period is called the *Middle Paleolithic* and lasted until about 40,000 years ago.

Although they looked different than modern man, having a much heavier brow, their brains were the same size. Their way of life was more advanced than that of earlier humans. They hunted, lived in caves and used a variety of stone tools. Like us, they buried their dead. Perhaps they had some concept of an afterlife, for at the grave of an old Neanderthal man, flowers had been placed with the body.

THE EMERGENCE OF MODERN MAN By about 100,000 BC, the first modern humans, *homo sapiens sapiens*, had emerged in southern Africa. The descendants of these people, indistinguishable from ourselves, moved into Europe and replaced the Neanderthals some 35,000 years ago. The period to about 12,000 years ago is

Europe During the Ice Age

Much of Europe was covered with glaciers during the Ice Age. It was freezing cold and only stunted plants, lichens and mosses could grow. The climate became warmer some 10,000 years ago and as the ice sheets melted, the sea level rose, changing coastlines.

known as the *Upper Paleolithic*, and much is known about it, especially in Europe.

These people lived together in cave entrances and rock shelters, or if there were no caves, they built large tents or huts, in which they had fires for heating and cooking. They hunted large animals such as mammoths, bison and reindeer, and gathered plants. They made tools from bone, antler and ivory, as well as stone. Apart from hunting, they used tools for a number of other tasks. They also invented the bow and arrow.

A reconstruction of what a community might have looked like in Upper Palaeolithic times. People either lived in caves or tents, such as these. Tents were made out of the skins of animals. The tents shown here are constructed on frames of mammoth bones. The woman on the left is pegging out a hide to let it dry before being used as a tent covering. The people are also wearing clothes made from animal hides. The temperature was much colder during this period so substantial clothing such as this would probably have been worn.

Hunting Weapons

Several new types of weapons came into use during the Stone Age, including the barbed harpoon and the spear. To throw spears a long distance, spear-throwers were used, which were attached to the hunters' wrists with leather thongs. The spearhead was placed on long wooden shafts whose bases fitted into the grooves of the throwers. Often these spear-throwers were beautifully carved with designs of animals.

Bone spearheads (1,2); barbed harpoons (3,4); harpoons attached to wooden shafts (5,6); double-headed harpoon (7); barbed spearhead (8).

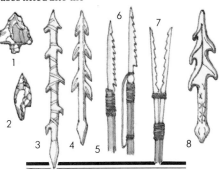

A wall painting from a cave at Lascaux in the Dordogne region of France, c. 15,000 BC. Bison, ibex, stags, horses and other animals were vividly depicted by the cave artists.

ART AND SCULPTURE The earliest known art was created by these Upper Paleolithic hunters. The walls of caves and rock shelters were painted with pictures of animals such as deer, bison and horses. People are seldom shown, although they were sometimes painted wearing masks, antlers and animal skins; it is possible that these scenes are connected with hunting rituals. From what is known of communities that still live by hunting, which is done mainly by young men, these paintings might also be connected with ceremonies celebrating the entry of young hunters into the adult hunting group. The paintings were made with natural color pigments crushed or ground from rocks or plants. Although cave paintings are known from elsewhere, many especially beautiful pictures are found in south west France and northern Spain.

These hunter-gatherers also engraved or carved animals and human figures in stone, ivory and bone antler. Whatever its original purpose, people still find the art of these ancient hunters very beautiful. Indeed, so many people have visited the caves at Lascaux in France that the paintings have started to decay, so a reconstruction has been created for people to visit.

The First Settlements
FARMERS OF THE NEAR EAST

The Spread of Agriculture

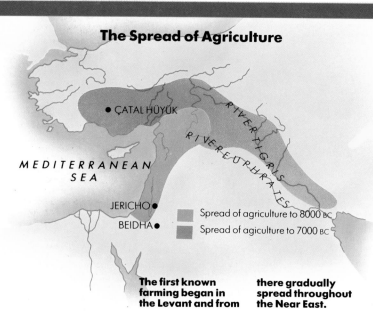

ÇATAL HÜYÜK

RIVER TIGRIS

RIVER EUPHRATES

MEDITERRANEAN SEA

JERICHO

BEIDHA

Spread of agriculture to 8000 BC
Spread of agiculture to 7000 BC

The first known farming began in the Levant and from **there gradually spread throughout the Near East.**

Around 10,000 BC the last Ice Age ended. As the ice sheets that had covered northern Europe receded, and temperatures rose, there were more places where people could live and there were more food resources. This meant that the population grew. It also meant that, in spite of the improved conditions, in some places there were probably too many people living from hunting and gathering, and food was becoming harder to get.

One of the most important discoveries now took place. People learned that they could grow their own plants and rear animals themselves. In learning to farm, mankind took the first great step in controlling the world he lived in.

Up till now, people had followed the animals as they moved in search of new grazing. Similarly they had gathered wild plants, though from experience they would have known where and when there were plants ready to be harvested.

Now people became settled farmers, living in one place where they cultivated their crops and reared their animals. The terms *agriculture* and *stock-breeding* are used to describe these activities. This period of early farming is called *Neolithic* (New Stone Age).

Agriculture first developed in the Near East, in the uplands and grasslands of modern Iran, Iraq, Turkey and the Levant, which includes Lebanon, Palestine and northern Syria.

We cannot be sure of exactly when people first began cultivating plants, but we do know that by 7000 BC, wheat, barley, peas and lentils were being grown in the Near East. Animals, such as goats, sheep and pigs, were also domesticated.

THE TOWN OF JERICHO In some places stock breeding and plant cultivation had started long before, as for example in the Jordan Valley at Jericho. This site was excavated in the 1950s by Dame Kathleen Kenyon and gradually she was able to piece together the town's history.

Here, in about 8000 BC, a fortified town covering some 10 acres developed. Inside the town's wall was a large circular stone tower which still stands to a height of almost 10 yards. The town was obviously wealthy enough to support a workforce to build the defensive wall and tower, and it is thought that this wealth probably came from trade.

The archaeologists there found *turquoise* from Sinai, *cowrie shells* from the Red Sea and *obsidian* from Turkey. Obsidian is a hard, black volcanic glass that was used for cutting. Because these precious objects came from elsewhere, we can be reasonably sure that the people of Jericho traded with other communities.

As time went by, a new group of people came to live here and they built rectangular shaped houses with plastered floors, which were often painted red.

One interesting discovery, which is thought to be connected to the worship of ancestors, was a group of human skulls. Faces of clay had been modeled on them and cowrie shells set into the eye sockets.

THE ECONOMY DEVELOPS Gradually in addition to farming, other specialized skills were developing. South of Jordan at Beidha workshops for various crafts and trades have been found. Tools, new materials and half-made objects of these ancient craftsmen and traders lay in their shops; one was a beadmaker, another a stonemason, and there was a butcher.

As we have seen, as people became settled farmers and food production increased, they were able to support some who did not work on the land. In this way *specialization* developed and the work of such craftsmen in turn stimulated trade between communities.

A good example of this process is the obsidian trade which played a part in the *economy* of the large village of Çatal Hüyük in Turkey, which you can see in the picture.

1 Around 8500 BC the first rock paintings in the Sahara appeared, showing wild, and later domestic animals. Around 7500 BC the first pottery appeared in the Sahara region.

2 The glaciers began to retreat c. 8300 BC, flooding lowland areas. Many new plants appeared that could be gathered by the hunter-gatherers. Around 6500 BC farming spread to the Balkans in southeast Europe, probably from Anatolia. Britain became separated from continental Europe by rising sea levels.

3 By 7500 BC farming had spread from western Asia to Pakistan. Also by this time, farming had developed independently in India. Farming villages had appeared in China by 6000 BC, and pigs and dogs had become domesticated. Rice cultivation began in China around 5000 BC.

4 The first evidence for plant cultivation in South America points to a date of 8500 BC. By 7500 BC crops were being cultivated in Mexico and the Upper Amazon region. Special grains for high altitudes began to be cultivated in Peru around 6300 BC, and potato cultivation began.

Çatal Hüyük

Çatal Hüyük is the largest known Neolithic site in the Near East, and dates from about 6000 to 5000 BC. It covered some 32 acres and about 5000 to 6000 people lived there.

It was the first community known to use *irrigation* to bring water to crops, and the people grew many different crops. They also made textiles and much attractive jewelry. The wealth came from obsidian, found nearby. It was prized for making axes, daggers and mirrors and was traded over long distances. The houses, made of mud, brick and wood, were built adjoining each other. People entered their houses from the flat roofs, along which they walked from one to another.

Some of the buildings seem to have been *shrines* or holy places for worshiping the gods. The walls were painted and there were bulls' heads modeled in plaster on the walls, perhaps representing a bull-god.

Left. This is a reconstruction of a funerary ritual in one of the many shrines that have been unearthed at Çatal Hüyük. The priestesses are disguised as vultures.

15

THE SPREAD OF FARMING TO EUROPE

Farming spread from Anatolia to the Balkans, that is south-east Europe, by about 6000 BC. Farming here was similar to that of the Near East as conditions were much the same. Wheat, barley, lentils and peas were grown and sheep, goats, pigs and cattle were bred by the people who lived here.

By 6200 BC there were farming villages in Sicily and southern Italy. These people lived in groups of huts which stood in large enclosures surrounded by ditches.

The new farming techniques spread only gradually further west along the Mediterranean coast. Here, communities of hunter-gatherers for whom fishing was also important, lived in caves and rock shelters. Even when they had started breeding sheep and goats people continued to hunt, fish and gather wild crops – probably because there were still plentiful supplies. But slowly cultivation increased and by about 5000 BC the first farming villages had developed in the south of France.

THE INFLUENCE OF CLIMATE Gradually farming techniques spread northwest, and crops and stock had to be adapted to the cooler, more temperate weather. In central Europe the rich loamy soil was easily cultivated and was well suited to agriculture; the nearby forests

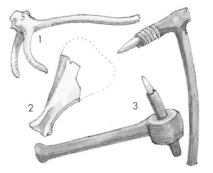

Although stone tools were still used, new woodworking tools for building and farming began to be made. Examples of these tools can be seen to the left as follows: a rake (1); a shovel made from a shoulder blade (2); small axes in wooden holders (3,4).

were ideal for pigs. In this environment which was very different to the hotter and dryer Near East, pig and cattle herding replaced sheep and goats.

HOUSING Not only farming techniques, but also houses, had to be adapted to a more rainy and cooler environment. The extensive forests provided plenty of timber for building. The villages of these farming people contained large longhouses which were sometimes as long as 50 yards. They were built of timber with thatched roofs and were usually divided into three parts. In the middle was the main living area; the cattle were kept in one end and the other was used for storage. The houses

were built in groups of two to five and each group had its own animal pens and rubbish pits.

Within two to three hundred years knowledge of farming had spread from central Europe to north-western Europe. We know this, because as well as the typical longhouses which in time were built from central Europe to the Netherlands, these people are also known for their distinctive lined pottery. Archaeologists call this early farming culture *Bandkeramik* after the pottery style first found in central Europe and later in the north and west.

As in the Near East, trade between different communities was carried out over long distances. Tombs in central Europe contained shells from the Aegean and the Adriatic as well as various stones not available locally.

NORTHERN EUROPE At the northern fringes of Europe, the hunter gatherer way of life continued for a long time because there was an abundance of food that could be gathered, hunted or fished. In general, farming was usually only adopted because there were no longer enough natural resources. In Denmark for instance, the disappearance of the oyster, which had been an important source of food in the spring and winter, led to the development of farming in order to provide food to replace it.

By about 4000 BC, farming was well established in Europe. Communities had increased in size, specialization of crafts developed and trading links expanded.

Styles of Pottery

Pottery is very important for helping archaeologists to understand the past. Different communities made distinctive styles of pottery, and as potsherds (broken pieces) are virtually indestructible, facts such as population movements, or length of habitation can be worked out by looking at pottery evidence. When people stay in one place there is more time to make pottery.

In antiquity, pottery was used for many purposes. Food storage and cooking were key among its uses.

Pottery was fired at very high temperatures in a kiln, after having been decorated with painted or engraved designs.

A painted vase from Yugoslavia (1); a Neolithic pot of a type known as 'clay flame' (2); pot with a face and a pedestal base from Hungary c. 4500 BC (3); a painted vase from Romania (4); Bandkeramik pot from Germany c. 4300 BC (5).

An early farming community in central Europe. The men on the left are making hurdles for fences and animal shelters. A longhouse is being re-thatched on the near left. Thatch was made from dried straw and laid on interwoven branches. The woman and child on the near left are making pottery with a banded decoration known as bandkeramik.

COPPER, GOLD AND THE DISCOVERY OF BRONZE

Early Metallurgy in Europe

Areas of copper/bronze metallurgy 6000 – 3000 BC
Areas of gold

Copper and gold were the earliest metals in use. This was probably because nuggets of these occur naturally and could easily be formed into objects by hammering or cutting with stones. At some point, ancient man realized that by heating metal ores, pure metal could be separated out. Once molten, metals could be cast. This was the beginning of metallurgy and this stage was achieved at different periods in different parts of the world.

Left. This is an Egyptian tomb painting depicting the melting of copper for the casting of a pair of large temple doors. It dates from 2000 BC. The furnaces are being blown by pot bellows. It is one of the earliest records of metalworking.

Above. A gold Hittite necklace, c. 1700–1500 BC.

The discovery of metals and the development of metalworking further extended our ancestors' ability to control their environment. The earliest metals to be used were copper and gold. These metals were sometimes found in rivers and the sand as attractive nuggets soft enough to be hammered flat and cut with stone tools. Archaeologists have found beads and other ornaments made this way, together with stone and bone objects in Neolithic graves.

THE DISCOVERY OF METAL ORES But as *alluvial* (river) and surface gold deposits are fairly rare, it was the discovery that metal bearing rocks or *ores* could be heated to extract pure metal, that marks the beginning of true *metallurgy* (the term used to describe the science of metals).

This discovery seems to have been made separately in different places. In western Asia and the Balkans it was around 7000 to 6000 BC and in the Far East, some time before 2000 BC. From these regions the techniques spread to other parts of Europe, Africa and Asia.

Some of the first pieces of hammered and worked copper objects were made in Turkey in about 7000 to 6000 BC at Çayonu, an ancient site which lay only about thirteen miles from a copper mine. The earliest known metal object to be cast in a mold is a copper mace-head from Can Hasan in Anatolia (Turkey). To cast objects, the heated metal was poured into shaped stone molds.

In Iran archaeologists have found traces of waste material from *crucibles*, and this evidence dates from about 4000 BC. Also found in Iran, and dating from about a thousand years later, were stone molds used for casting copper tools. Evidence such as this tells us that both Turkey and Iran were early centers of copper mining and working, and would have been major suppliers of copper to other areas.

From archaeological remains and from written evidence, we know that copper was mined in ancient Dilmun, now Bahrain, and was exported to the cities of southern Mesopotamia and the Indus Valley people. The Egyptians got their copper from Sinai and from southern Palestine, where at Timna, near Eilat, copper mines and

Above. Necklaces and headbands from the early dynastic Royal Tombs of Ur in Sumer c. 2500 BC. The gold beads are made from a bitumen core and covered with gold foil.

Early Mining and Smelting

Above are shown early miners extracting ores. The vertical shafts could extend to 13 yards in depth. Light could always be provided either by lamps or by daylight. The miner on the right is shown digging with the aid of a deer's antler which is being used as a pick. His companion to the right collects together the ore and puts it in a crude net which is then hauled to the top of the shaft.

The diagram at the top right shows an ancient copper mine that was worked using tunnels that were horizontal to the hillside.

In this Bronze Age copper mine, miners used bronze picks to excavate tunnels.

They then used fire and water to break up the ore and bring it to the surface.

furnaces have been found. Later, they imported copper from Cyprus; the name 'Cyprus' literally means the 'copper' island.

Although there was copper in the desert to the east of the Nile there were also the gold mines of the Wadi Hammamat. An ancient map on papyrus shows the mines to which the pharoahs sent large expeditions to bring back gold. Nubia, in the south, was another source of Egypt's gold.

THE BRONZE AGE Metals were at first used for ornament, but the discovery of bronze provided a much harder metal which could be used for weapons and tools. Bronze is an *alloy*, a mixture of copper and tin. Other alloys had been used, such as copper and arsenic, but true bronze was widely used in the Near East by about 2000 BC. It is possible that the tin came from as far as Cornwall, although some came from Afghanistan. The period when both stone and copper were used is called the *Chalcolithic* (meaning copper and stone) and was followed by the *Bronze Age*.

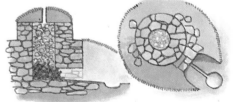

A shaft furnace used for smelting copper, seen from the side and above. Once smelted, the molten metal ran off through a hole in the side into an ingot.

In 4000 BC most of Europe was still covered by forest, but within 1000 years, much land had been cleared for farming. As in the Near East and elsewhere, the numbers of people grew with the spread of farming.

Farming techniques had gradually improved. The plough meant that more ground could be cultivated, which increased the supply of food. As metal became more widely used, farming implements became more efficient. For example, metal blades gave a sharper cutting edge to the *sickle*, which meant that more grain could be harvested.

THE MOUND PEOPLE Everything that is known about the prehistoric people of Europe comes from their *material remains*. As there is no written evidence, we do not know what the various groups of people called themselves. Archaeologists however, have given names to some of them.

One group, who lived in Denmark over 3,000 years ago, is called the *Mound People* after their many round burial mounds. Much more is known about the customs of the Mound People than most other groups. This is because they were buried in boggy ground, which lacks oxygen and so their bodies and belongings have been preserved through time.

The women wore skirts and blouses, some of which were embroidered. The jewelry was of bronze, gold and silver, and included bracelets, arm rings, and finger rings. Most of the weapons were made of bronze and included swords and daggers. One of the coffins contained a vessel of birch bark which had held a mixture of beer and apple wine. Birch bark was also used for boxes, and ash wood was used to make folding seats.

Archaeologists have excavated the houses of people who lived next to lakes in Switzerland, northern Italy and eastern France. Some of these houses were very large, with up to 50 people living in them. They were rectangular in shape and were made from wood. They were thatched with reeds from the lakes.

THE MYSTERY OF THE MEGALITHS In Britain, Ireland and northwest France, there are the remains of monuments, whose functions are not always well understood. They are called *megaliths* because of the very large stones used to build them.

Some of these structures formed part of a burial complex, while others seem to have been used for ceremonial purposes, perhaps linked with the seasons and astronomy. But whatever their purpose, they could only have been built by well established and well organized communities: it has been estimated that it took about 15,700 manhours to build the *longbarrows* at West Kennet in England.

One of the best preserved megalith constructions is Stonehenge. During the Bronze Age, about 1300 BC, an earlier ceremonial center was made larger to create the site as we know it today. The huge stones that can still be seen, were set up, having been brought from the Marlborough Downs, about 17 miles away. The people who did this are called Beaker people.

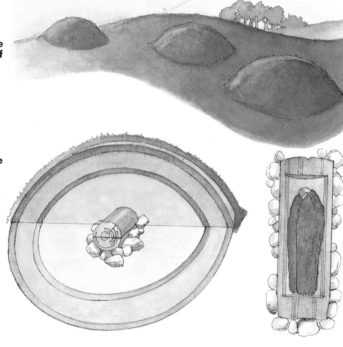

The reconstruction to the right shows a typical burial mound, as used by the Mound People of Denmark. Many mound burials have survived because of the bog conditions.

When these people died they were wrapped in oxhide skins and then buried in oak coffins, such as the coffin shown at the far right of the diagram. They were buried with their clothes, jewelry, weapons and tools.

Above. A reconstruction of Stonehenge as it might have appeared during its construction. The labor and effort that must have been involved in the building of this ritual site was immense. Sarsen blocks each weighing an average of 28.6 tons, were brought from the Marlborough Downs some 17.4 miles to the north. Their mode of transport was probably sledges using rollers and ropes, and it would have taken something like 1000 people to haul just one stone. Bluestones were the other type of stone used for construction, and these were quarried from the Prescelly Mountains in Wales, over 130 miles away. The stones were raised into position by putting the lower edge over the posthole, and pulled upright using ropes.

Right. West Kennet (in Wiltshire, UK) is a Neolithic mound which has megalithic burial chambers at one end. It was used for 1000 years until c. 2500 BC, and was probably linked to death rituals. The remains of over 40 people have been found there.

Megalithic Tombs

NORTH SEA

STONEHENGE ●
WEST KENNET ●

ATLANTIC OCEAN

■ Early tombs c. 4500–4000 BC
■ Spread of tombs 4000 BC–2000 BC

Megalithic tombs were used in many different parts of the world, but the main development occurred in western Europe during the Neolithic period.

THE DEVELOPMENT OF WRITING

We all take writing for granted, but as with farming and metalworking, it is not something that people have always done, but it *is* another immensely important human invention.

The first known writing system was developed in Mesopotamia, the land between the Tigris and Euphrates Rivers, in what is today, Iraq. The earliest forms of this system date from around 3200 to 2800 BC. As the first examples of writing are of numbers of objects only, it seems that writing originated from the need to keep accounts and records.

PICTOGRAMS At first picture signs, called *pictograms* were used to indicate objects. A picture of a head or of grain, meant quite simply 'head' or 'grain.' Gradually this system expanded to suggest objects or ideas that could not be put into pictures. In this way, for instance, the Sumerian sign for 'mouth' came to also mean 'speak.' Another way of expressing actions or ideas was to combine two signs to mean a third; thus the sign for

mouth and food was combined to mean 'eat.'

An important step was taken when a picture was used to represent the sound of the name and not the object it showed. These are called *sound signs*; for example, if we were using such a system, pictures of an eye and a saw, would represent the sounds 'I saw' in English.

CUNEIFORM WRITING Because there was plenty of clay, people wrote on wet clay tablets with a sharpened reed or stylus. The tablet was left to dry in the sun. Gradually the picture forms became more abstract and a stylus with a triangular tip was used. This left wedge shaped impressions in the clay, hence the writing is called *cuneiform* from the Latin meaning 'wedge shaped.'

The cuneiform script was invented by the Sumerians. Later, other people in the Near East used this script to write their own very different languages. Akkadian, which was the earliest Semitic language, and the Indo-European Hittite, were both written in cuneiform. Similarly, today all European languages are written in the same script that the Romans once used, although the languages are different.

OTHER WRITING SYSTEMS As you can see from the map, several different writing systems developed in various parts of the world. In Ancient Egypt they used a picture script which we call *hieroglyphic* in which the pictures represented both sounds and ideas. The Egyptians wrote with a brush and ink on *papyrus*, which was similar to paper and was made from the stem of the papyrus plant.

The first Chinese writing was also derived from pictures and was written on bones. Later, the Chinese invented paper. At about the same time that the Akkadians were writing in cuneiform, the people of the Indus Valley used a script that cannot yet be read.

All of these systems were complex and took many years to learn. Most people could not read or write, so that writing was done by a small group of *scribes* who were trained in the temple or palace schools. Around 1000 BC a much simpler form of writing emerged. This is called *alphabetic* and was first used by the Phoenicians. The Greeks adopted this system in which words are made from individual letters which stand for sounds. This is the system that the Romans borrowed and adapted and that we now use.

How Papyrus was Made

Papyrus was made from the stem of the papyrus plant which grew in the Nile delta. The diagrams below show how papyrus was actually made.

To form scrolls, several pieces of papyrus were stuck together. Papyrus continued in use until it was replaced by parchment, which was invented by the Hellenistic city of Pargamon.

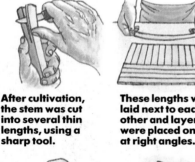

After cultivation, the stem was cut into several thin lengths, using a sharp tool.

These lengths were laid next to each other and layers were placed on top at right angles.

This shows the papyrus plant before cultivation.

A piece of cloth was laid on top and was hammered gently to break down the fibers.

The papyrus was left to dry slightly, then rubbed smooth with a stone.

Below. This map shows the origin and development of early scripts. Most of the early scripts were pictographic, hieroglyphic or cuneiform.

An early Akkadian cylinder seal impression c. 2334–2000 BC. Seals such as this were worn for adornment and for sealing and signing documents, storage jars, etc.

Often they were passed down in families. The inscription reads: 'Ubil-Eshtar, brother of the king; Kalki, the scribe, is your servant.'

The Spread of Writing

GREECE

MYCENAE●
KNOSSOS●

ANATOLIA

●UGARIT

GIZA●

EGYPT

●URUK

ARABIA

●MOHENJO-DARA

INDIA

ANYANG●

CHINA

INDIAN OCEAN

3500 BC	Earliest writing in Mesopotamia
3000 BC	Writing develops in Egypt
2500–1700 BC	Scripts appear in the Indus Valley
1700–1200 BC	Linear A and B develop in Greece
1500–600 BC	Hieroglyphic and cuneiform scripts in Asia Minor and northern Syria
1400 BC	Writing develops in China
1400 BC	Early alphabets in Syria and Palestine

Cuneiform Writing

Cuneiform literally means 'wedge-shaped writing.' It was written on damp clay tablets with a reed pen (as shown below). It was invented by the Sumerians and later adapted for Akkadian and other languages. It was used in the Near East until it was displaced by the Aramaic script. Cuneiform tablets have been found at many sites in western Asia and neighboring lands.

Below. This is the Rosetta Stone, inscribed by Egyptian priests in 196 BC. It provided the key to deciphering Egyptian hieroglyphics, since the inscription is written in two forms of Egyptian and in ancient Greek.

The chart below shows part of the developing stages of cuneiform from the original incised drawings of recognizable objects to more abstract strokes.

The tablet above is an early administrative tablet from Jemdet Nasr c. 2900 BC. It is written in cuneiform and lists areas of fields and crops.

BIRD	WALK/STAND	DONKEY	WATER	FISH

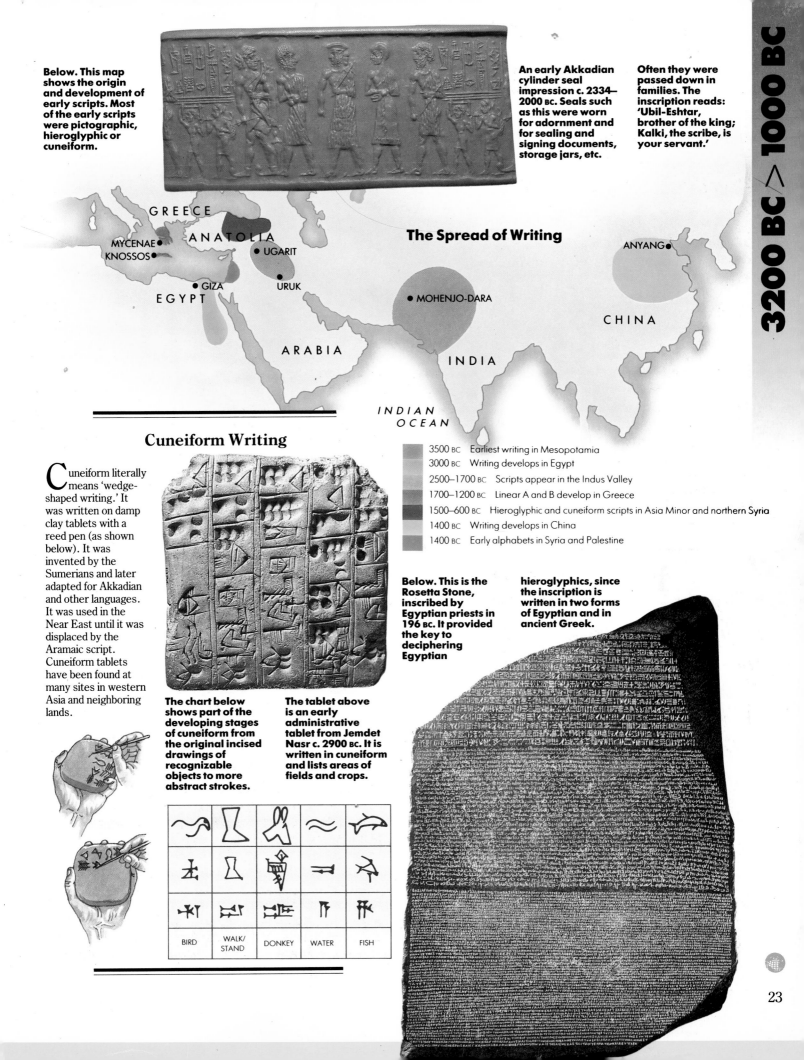

The First Civilizations
THE EMERGENCE OF CITIES

The first known cities were built by the Sumerians in about 3500 BC. The land of Sumer lay in what is today southern Iraq. This region, between the Tigris and Euphrates Rivers, is also called *Mesopotamia*, from the Greek, meaning 'the land between the rivers.'

Elsewhere, urban civilization, that is, the civilization of cities, also developed next to great rivers. The Nile, the Indus and the Yellow River in China were all, independently, early centers of urban life.

Why did these early cities develop next to rivers? Why are the first cities not found in the regions where people had farmed since 7000 BC? To try and understand why urban life emerged in the river valleys, let us look at early Sumer.

FARMING IN SUMER Before the Sumerians adopted agriculture they already had good supplies of food including fish from the rivers, wildfowl from the marshes and the fruit of the date-palm. We do not know precisely when these people began to farm, but by 4000 BC this region had become more productive than the earlier upland centers of farming.

One reason for this was the rich soil. Each year the rivers flooded the plain and left a layer of fertile soil brought down from the hills: this is called alluvium. There was, however, little rain and once the floodwaters receded, the earth dried out under the hot sun. No

Left. This white marble mask, almost life-sized, comes from the temple precinct of Eanna at Warka (Uruk).

Below. This shows the peace side from the Standard of Ur. Thought to be the sounding box of a musical instrument, this object has both peaceful and warlike scenes on either side of each other. The original wooden box was covered with bitumen and overlaid with a colored mosaic of shell, lapis lazuli and red limestone. It dates from 2500 BC.

matter how rich the soil, nothing grows without water. If water could be led from the river to the soil, then crops would grow, and this is exactly what was done.

We call it irrigation farming and it is still used today. Water is fed to the fields from a dam or river, along artificial canals. Fertile soil and water provided plenty of food, which meant that more people survived and multiplied. The irrigation system itself required a degree

Early Cities

1 In 3200 BC Egypt was unified and the First Dynasty appeared. In 2800 BC construction work was begun on the pyramids of Giza, and the era of the Old Kingdom began. The Old Kingdom came to an end in 2100 BC, and the Middle Kingdom commenced in 2040 BC.

2 The first wheeled vehicles appeared in Europe in 3200 BC. Megalithic monuments become prominent in Britain and northwest France. The European Bronze Age began c. 2300 BC. By 2000 BC the main phase of building had begun at Stonehenge, and the palace centers of Minoan Crete had appeared.

3 By 3000 BC the plough was in use in China and farming had begun in Korea. Silk weaving in China begins and the first bronze objects start to appear. The Indus Valley civilization, with great centers at Mohenjo-Dara and Harappa, had developed by 2500 BC.

4 By 3500 BC the llama was being used in Peru as a domestic pack animal; cotton was being grown in southern Peru and textiles were being made. From 2800–2300 BC, villages appear in the Amazon region, temple mounds are found in Peru, and the earliest ceramics appear in central America.

of organization and cooperation between communities. New canals had to be built and existing ones left clear. Also, as the network of waterways expanded, so communications increased. The rivers and canals acted like roads, with people traveling along them by boat.

BEGINNINGS OF SOCIETY Often there was more food grown than people could eat: this is called a surplus. It could either be stored to feed people after a poor harvest or it could be exchanged for goods not available locally. It could also feed specialists who no longer lived by farming but by their crafts or trading.

All these factors meant that society became more complex and small farming villages gradually became larger centers which had to be organized, protected and governed.

We do not know exactly how rulers, armies and government emerged. It is possible that as disputes over boundaries became more common between opposing tribes, a warlord was appointed. In time, such leaders would have become kings in charge of large armies.

Because the earliest writings seem to record the delivery of food to temples, it is thought that the temples functioned like government departments, collecting taxes and organizing food supplies. Archaeologists have excavated some of these cities which had developed by about 3000 BC.

Some of the first cities appeared on the flat river plain of the Tigris and Euphrates Rivers. Trade was extremely important to people living in this area, and all the major early towns are to be found on the rivers. The

Sumerians traded over impressive distances — to Afghanistan, the Lebanon, Anatolia and Persia — and brought back goods such as timber, lapis lazuli, precious stones, and metal ores.

Above. A libation vase from Uruk c. 3000 BC. It is one of the earliest examples of Sumerian art where wild heroes of the countryside are shown protecting animals.

THE SUMERIANS

Most people in the first Sumerian towns were farmers. Each town or city lay at the center of an area of cultivation. Barley, linseed and sesame were some of the main crops, as were date palms which grew in orchards along the river and canal banks. Oxen, pigs and sheep grazed on the land.

HOUSES AND TEMPLES At first houses were made of reeds, and indeed the Marsh Arabs of Iraq still live in houses of an almost identical style. In time however, they learned to build with mud bricks which they strengthened with straw and dried in the sun. In an area of little rainfall such houses can last for many years.

The most important buildings in the cities were the temples. The Sumerians believed that the gods who ruled the world, lived on mountains, and it is thought that the high terraced *ziggurats*, or temple towers, reflect this tradition. It was their belief that mankind existed to serve the gods and goddesses who had to be looked after like kings and

queens. Priests served them in their temples and people brought food and clothes with which to feed and dress the gods. The priests were rich and powerful as they looked after all the wealth belonging to the gods.

The Sumerian cities were independent city states ruled by their kings who also headed the army. The temple priests administered the cities, collected taxes and were usually in charge of clearing the canals. Sometimes one city was stronger and controlled other cities, but until the time of Sargon of Agade there was no large unified state in the region.

SARGON OF AGADE In 2340 BC the first great age of the Sumerians ended when Sargon took control of the region. His capital was north of Sumer at Agade which has not yet been discovered. Sargon spoke Akkadian which is not related to the Sumerian language but is the ancestor of modern Arabic and is a Semitic language. Although Sargon led his armies to Anatolia, the Levant and Syria, his 'Empire' was shortlived

Near right. This bronze head is thought to be of Sargon of Agade. It was found at Nineveh in Assyria and dates from 2300—2000 BC. **Far right.** The Ziggurat at Ur was the core of the sacred precinct. It was dedicated to Nanna, the Moon God. Ziggurats were first built by Sumerians in the third millenium BC. They were monumental structures in the form of stepped towers, at the summit of which was a shrine. Ziggurats represented the sacred mountains where men communicated with the gods. The Ziggurat at Ur is the best preserved of all those that remain standing today.

Above. This plan of the world, with Babylon on the River Euphrates as the center, was drawn to illustrate the campaigns of Sargon of Agade. According to later traditions, Sargon campaigned as far north as Anatolia and to the Levant in the west.

The Royal Tombs of Ur

The city of Ur became one of the most important cities in Sumer during the third millenium BC. It was excavated between 1923–1934 by the British archaeologist, Leonard Woolley, and has since become famous for its royal tombs and ziggurat.

There are a total of 16 royal burials, and those of the greatest kings of Ur were located close to the ziggurat. The rulers were accompanied in their tombs by their retainers, and by some of the most beautiful jewelry and other objects which survive from ancient times.

A piece of jewelry and a dagger sheath from the Royal Tombs of Ur.

and did not continue beyond his great grandson. Nevertheless, for the first time, the whole of Mesopotamia had been one political unity.

After the overthrow of Sargon's dynasty there was a revival of Sumerian civilization and for about a century from c.2100 BC, Ur became the most important Sumerian city. The Royal Tombs of Ur show how wealthy these people were. During this time the temples were rebuilt and were even larger and more impressive than earlier temples.

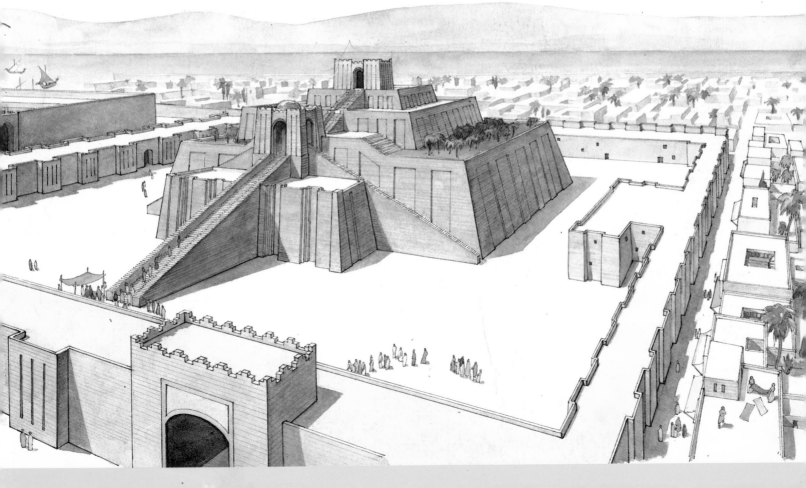

ANCIENT EGYPT

Egypt has been described as 'The gift of the Nile,' for without the river, nothing would grow in the valley, which is bounded by desert on either side. But the annual flood made the land fertile, and by 5000 BC there were people living in farming villages along the river. Gradually two kingdoms developed, Lower Egypt in the north, and Upper Egypt in the south. They were unified by the first *pharaoh* Menes around 3200 BC.

THE PHARAOHS The Egyptians believed that their king was a living god who had control over all aspects of life, including the Nile floods. The king lived in a palace called 'Per'ao' meaning 'the Great House.' The title *pharoah* comes from this word.

During his lifetime, the Pharaoh was believed to be the falcon headed sun-god, *Horus*. At death he became the mummified god of the underworld, *Osiris*. Because the Egyptians believed that death was the beginning of an afterlife, they regarded tombs as houses of eternity into which were placed everything needed for the next life.

The *pyramids* were the tombs of the Old Kingdom rulers, but because robbers stole from them, later pharaohs were buried in tombs hidden in the Valley of the Kings. But most of these were also robbed, except for the tomb of the boy-king Tutankhamun. This unplundered tomb was found by Howard Carter in 1922. There was so much treasure that it took several years for the tomb to be fully excavated. The many beautiful objects are now in the Cairo museum, but the king's *mummy* has been left in the tomb.

THE PRACTICE OF MUMMIFICATION People were mummified to preserve their bodies for the afterlife. After their intestines, lungs and liver and heart were removed and placed in *canopic jars*, the body was placed in *natron* for 40 days and then wrapped in resin-soaked bandages. Scientists and archaeologists sometimes study mummies to find out more about the health of the Egyptians.

The people and actions depicted in wall-paintings found in the tombs, which have been preserved in the dry desert conditions, give us a great deal of information about the Egyptians.

EGYPTIAN FARMING Most people lived in villages in flatroofed mud brick houses, farming the land close to the river. They grew wheat, barley and many types of vegetables, including peas, beans and lentils. Although cattle were raised and there were various domestic birds like ducks and geese, most people seldom ate meat but got their protein from lentils, eggs and fish.

When the land was flooded, they worked for the king, building pyramids, temples or palaces. As well as farmers, there were craftsmen such as jewelers, masons, carpenters, sculptors, painters, some of whom worked for the great nobles or the king. Some craftsmen worked only on the royal tombs, which began to be prepared at the beginning of each pharaoh's reign.

DEVELOPMENT OF A WRITING SYSTEM The Egyptians were one of the first people to use a writing system: it is called *hieroglyphic*. Law cases, letters, medical and magical texts, stories, poems and hymns, all survive on *papyri*. These help to give us a picture of life and events. From the hymns and funerary texts we know that the Egyptians worshipped many gods.

The sun god *Re'* was also the falcon-headed Horus, the living Pharaoh, whose mother was *Isis* and whose father was *Osiris*. Isis and Osiris were also brother and sister. *Seth*, the god of storms, violence and lord of the desert was also their brother. *Hathor* the cow-goddess represented music, dancing and love.

Some gods were linked to places such as *Hapi* the god of the Nile or *Ptah*, the god of craftsmen and god of Memphis.

Ancient Egypt

MEDITERRANEAN SEA

GIZA
MEMPHIS
EGYPT
RED SEA
THEBES
ASWAN
RIVER NILE
BUHEN

The region controlled by Egypt shifted considerably throughout its history, but at its greatest extent Egypt extended as far as the Euphrates River. Despite shifts in its boundaries during some 3000 years, for the most part Egypt controlled the lands to the east of the Nile to the Red Sea, and on the west it bordered with Libya.

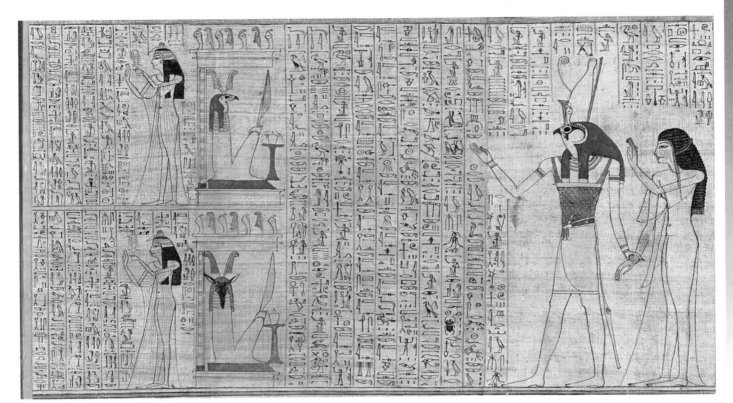

Above. This scene comes from the Book of the Dead, one of which was placed in each person's coffin.

Above. The tomb of Sennufer who was the royal gardener. The two people depicted are Sennufer and his wife. The tomb is most unusual in having the entire ceiling painted as a vine with hanging grapes. It dates from the 18th Dynasty.

Above and Left. This statue and frieze both depict Osiris, the Egyptian god of the Dead. At death, Egyptian pharaohs were believed to become Osiris. He is shown here carrying the crook and flail which were symbols of kingship in Egypt.

Egyptian Arts and Crafts

Though most Egyptians were farmers, an important minority worked as craftsmen.

Painters and sculptors had to obey some very strict rules in their art. They had to draw everything to the right proportions, and only show people in certain poses. This was because a picture in a tomb was supposed to 'come alive' in the next world when the priests had said the right prayers and spells. The scenes shown were then believed to go on happening forever.

THE GOLDEN AGE OF EGYPT

Egypt's very long history is divided into three periods. These are called the Old, Middle and New Kingdoms. In the Old Kingdom (c. 2686 – 2181 BC) powerful pharaohs sent expeditions to Sinai for turquoise and copper from which they made marvelous jewelry and ornaments. They also traded with the Lebanon for cedarwood which they used to build boats. In time the local nobles became more and more powerful and rivalry between the regions resulted in chaos which brought the Old Kingdom to an end.

THE MIDDLE KINGDOM Egypt was reunited under a king from Thebes, Mentuhotpe, in 2040 BC, and this marked the beginning of the Middle Kingdom. This period also ended in confusion brought about by the arrival of the Hyksos. These people had entered Egypt from Syria from about 1674 BC, and had managed to assert their power over Egypt. The Egyptians fought with the Hyksos and eventually drove them out of the country. Egypt now entered her most powerful and wealthy era – the period of the New Kingdom.

THE NEW KINGDOM During this period Egypt controlled much of Syria and Palestine and also Nubia to the south. Tribute from the subject states and gold from Nubia made Egypt the richest nation in the ancient world.

Throughout the period of the New Kingdom, the

The Tomb of Tutankhamun

Tutankhamun's tomb was discovered in 1922. Although ancient robbers had left some disorder, the tomb was virtually unplundered and was full of beautiful objects.

In the burial chamber, within four golden shrines, lay the heavy stone sarcophagus. Inside were three coffins, the innermost of solid gold, 1 in. thick and exquisitely decorated.

The dried, embalmed body of Tutankhamun was wrapped in bandages. Over his face was a superb gold funerary mask, decorated with precious stones and glass.

Right. The goddess Isis on the inside of the door of a golden shrine. Isis has winged arms to receive the dead. Far right. The golden coffin belonging to Tutankhamun. Below. A funerary bedhead in the form of a cheetah, from one of the beds in the antechamber of Tutankhamun's tomb.

pharaohs ruled from Thebes. Instead of pyramids which were visible and could be plundered, the pharaohs were buried in tombs cut out of the rock.

The area used for burial was called the Valley of the Kings, and it lies on the west bank of the Nile. It was here that Howard Carter discovered the unplundered tomb of Tutankhamun in 1922. Although he was not an important pharaoh, it took three years for archaeologists to excavate and record the immense riches of his tomb.

EGYPT UNDER THREAT Although still prosperous, towards the end of the New Kingdom Egypt's borders became threatened. Early in the thirteenth century BC, the Egyptians, under Ramesses II, fought the Hittites at the battle of Qaddesh. The result was indecisive, but Ramesses had his victory recorded on temple reliefs which still exist today.

In about 1200 BC there was turmoil in the countries bordering the Mediterranean. Troy and the Mycenaean cities of Greece were destroyed. The Hittite Empire collapsed suddenly and the cities of the Levant were laid waste. Finally, Egypt was attacked by groups of raiders called the Sea People. Twice the Egyptians defeated them and saved their country from invasion. But already Egypt's period of greatness was over. After the New Kingdom rival kings ruled from different cities and civil war broke out.

The Egyptian Army

During the Old Kingdom, the army was more like a militia, composed of contingents from the different 'nomes' or regions. It consisted entirely of light and heavy infantry. Later, mercenaries were recruited from Nubia and Libya, and they formed the greater part of the army.

In the Middle Kingdom, the army began to be recruited. Although each nome provided a quarter of the recruits, they were now permanent soldiers. There were still mercenaries, but far fewer than there had been formerly. This too was an infantry army of spearmen and archers.

Following the expulsion of the

An Egyptian soldier of the New Kingdom.

Hyksos, the army of the New Kingdom was quite different,

both in composition and in equipment. The nomes still provided their contingents for the regular army, but after a period of service, others took the place of these men so that there was now a trained reserve. The Hyksos had introduced the chariot and new weapons and equipment. There were now mounted forces as well as infantry. Armor was worn and the composite bow and a new form of axe were used. A few mercenaries were used at the beginning of the New Kingdom, but by the 20th Dynasty the Egyptian element in the army had again decreased.

The Tombs of the Valley of the Kings

On the west bank of the Nile, some miles from Thebes, in the 'Land of the Dead', have been found the tombs of 62 rulers. The desolate valley was chosen so that the tombs would remain hidden. In fact, only the tomb of Tutankhamun

remained virtually intact.

In order to keep the position of the tomb secret, the funerary temples for the worship of the dead rulers were built elsewhere. The most impressive of the tombs is that of Seti I, and it is illustrated below.

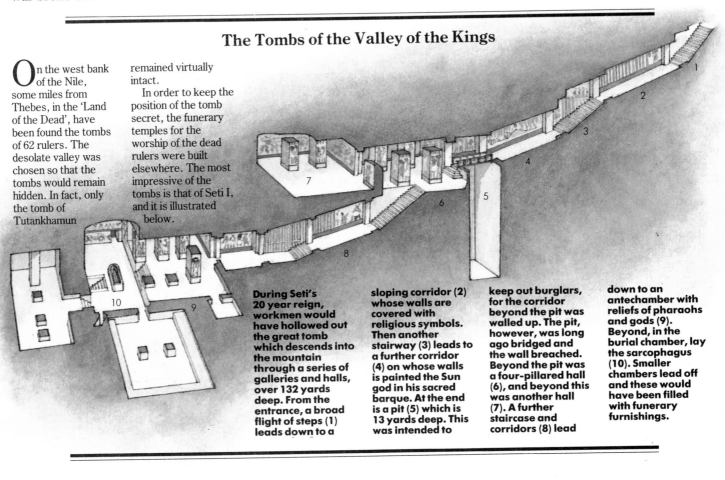

During Seti's 20 year reign, workmen would have hollowed out the great tomb which descends into the mountain through a series of galleries and halls, over 132 yards deep. From the entrance, a broad flight of steps (1) leads down to a

sloping corridor (2) whose walls are covered with religious symbols. Then another stairway (3) leads to a further corridor (4) on whose walls is painted the Sun god in his sacred barque. At the end is a pit (5) which is 13 yards deep. This was intended to

keep out burglars, for the corridor beyond the pit was walled up. The pit, however, was long ago bridged and the wall breached. Beyond the pit was a four-pillared hall (6), and beyond this was another hall (7). A further staircase and corridors (8) lead

down to an antechamber with reliefs of pharaohs and gods (9). Beyond, in the burial chamber, lay the sarcophagus (10). Smaller chambers lead off and these would have been filled with funerary furnishings.

KNOSSOS AND THE MINOAN CIVILIZATION

According to Greek legend, King Minos of Crete took an annual *tribute* from Athens of seven young men and seven girls. They were sacrificed to the *Minotaur*, a creature half-bull and half-man. The Minotaur lived in a maze under the palace of Knossos called the *labyrinth*.

The hero Theseus, whose father was the King of Athens, was selected as one of the seven youths. In Crete, Ariadne, the daughter of Minos, fell in love with Theseus. She gave him a ball of thread with which he was able to find his way out of the labyrinth after he had killed the Minotaur.

We do not know whether Minos was a real king or a mythical ruler, but such legendary stories do not seem as strange as they once did, before the long lost ancient civilization of Crete was discovered at the beginning of this century.

THE EXCAVATION OF KNOSSOS In March 1900 Arthur Evans, a wealthy scholar began excavations at Knossos. Gradually an extraordinarily rich and lively world was revealed. Evans called this civilization *Minoan*, after King Minos.

The palace at Knossos was built in about 2000 BC on the site of an earlier village. Other palaces have been found to the east of Knossos on the coast, at Mallia, and in the south of the island at Phaestos. There was also a palace in the east, at Zakro.

The palaces were several stories high with large rooms, and they were built around central courtyards. The royal apartments were painted with scenes of courtly life and naturalistic plants and animals. As well as being royal residences, the palaces were centers for the administration of the area.

Basement storerooms or *magazines* housed the surplus produce of grain, oil, wine and honey in stone boxes and large jars called *pithoi*. Craftsmen also worked at the palaces making beautiful jewelry and pottery.

Many paintings and engravings have been found of bull-leaping ceremonies, which probably took place in the palace courtyards. Young men and women would grasp the bull's horns and somersault over the animal.

The Minoans did not build temples, but worshiped the great mother goddess. They also had shrines to the snake goddess in their houses.

Early Aegean Civilization

GREECE · AEGEAN SEA · MYCENAE · CRETE · KNOSSOS · ZAKRO · PHAESTOS · MALLIA

Early civilization of Greece up to the Bronze Age

Left. A fresco of a woman from the Palace at Knossos c. 1500 BC.
Below. A reconstruction of the palace center at Knossos. Minoan palaces were both royal residences and the centers of government.

Above. Crete was first settled around 6000 BC. By 3000 BC larger settlements had begun to develop. From the period 2000–1700 BC, four palaces appeared on the island — at Phaestos, Mallia, Zakro, and the most famous of them all, at Knossos.

Left. This shows the fresco of the dolphins in the so-called Queen's apartments at Knossos. The fresco dates from c. 1500 BC. Minoan artists painted in a flowing and naturalistic style, frequently depicting plants and animals.

Above. This fresco depicts a bull-leaper in the act of somersaulting over the bull's back. There appears to have been a cult in Minoan Crete linked to the bull. It is thought that the bull-leaping took place in the large courtyard at the palace. In Minoan art, women are shown in white and men in red. So, you can see here that the bull-leaper is in fact a man. The fresco dates from 1500 BC and is 28 inches tall.

The Minoans also had settlements on the islands of Thera and Kythera. From Cretan objects found in Egypt and elsewhere in the Near East, we know that Crete traded with these lands. Large houses with colourful paintings and household objects have been found on Thera. One very interesting painting shows a naval expedition setting out to sea.

The Minoan writing system, called *Linear A*, has not yet been deciphered; it was used from about 1900 BC to 1450 BC.

Another script, *Linear B* was found at Knossos and was used from about 1450 to 1400 BC. The palaces and towns of Crete had been destroyed, probably by an earthquake, and abandoned in about 1450 BC.

Knossos however, was reoccupied for some fifty years by a new group of people from the Greek mainland. They adapted the Cretan Linear A script to write their own language.

TROY AND THE MYCENAEAN WORLD

The people from the Greek mainland who occupied Knossos in about 1450 BC are called Mycenaeans, after the town of Mycenae in southern Greece.

THE TROJAN WAR Homer's great poem, the *Iliad*, tells the story of the Greek expedition against Troy, led by King Agamemnon of Mycenae and other kings to recapture Helen. She was the beautiful wife of King Menelaus of Sparta, and had been abducted by the Trojan prince, Paris, whose father, Priam, was the king of Troy. The Trojan war lasted for 10 years and only ended when the Greeks used a trick to get into the city. They pretended to give the Trojans a gift of a wooden horse. Once the horse was in the city, the Greek soldiers hidden inside it broke out of the horse's body and attacked the Trojans.

This story was thought to be only legend, but in 1868 Heinrich Schliemann, who had made his fortune from trade, set out to find Troy. The site was identified as Hissarlik in Turkey, where a town was discovered which had existed from the early Bronze Age to the Roman era.

LEARNING ABOUT MYCENAE Homer's poems also include traditions about Mycenae, describing the city as 'rich in gold.' Although the poems were written at a much later date, about 800 BC, the information would have been passed down *orally*, by word of mouth. Schliemann's discoveries at Troy led him to excavate Mycenae, and he found remains of a war-like people which bore out Homer's descriptions.

The late Bronze Age Mycenaean civilization existed from about 1600 BC to 1150 BC. There were a number of

The wooden horse of Troy shown in relief on a Greek terra cotta amphora c. 670 BC. The story of how the Greeks tricked the Trojans after the 10-year long siege of the city is famous. It was Odysseus, the hero of Homer's great epic poem, the *Odyssey*, who devised the plan to get inside the city walls. The Greek fleet sailed away, leaving a huge wooden horse standing on the shore. The unsuspecting Trojans thought that this marked an end to the war and hauled the horse inside the city walls. But at midnight, the Greeks who were hiding inside the belly of the horse crept out. They opened the gates of Troy to let in the men from the Greek fleet, which had returned to Troy under the cover of darkness. The Greeks then destroyed Troy and Helen was reunited with her husband, Menelaus, king of Sparta.

small kingdoms, each with its central palace or *citadel*. These had often started as hillside villages which only later developed great fortifications.

At Mycenae, the huge walls were built around 1300 BC and extended in 1250 BC, when conditions were becoming increasingly troubled. Other towns such as Tiryns and Gla were also surrounded by immense walls. This type of wall in which huge stones were used, is called *Cyclopaean*, after the Cyclops, the giants, thought by the Greeks to have built the walls.

MYCENAEAN PALACES The rooms of the palaces were arranged around courtyards. The floors and walls were plastered and painted, often with scenes of daily life. The most important room in each palace was the *megaron*, a large hall with a central hearth and a roof supported on four wooden columns.

These palaces had many store rooms for produce and equipment. As elsewhere, the palace also had craft workshops producing beautiful ivory, gold and other objects. The influence of Cretan craftsmanship is clear, especially in the wall painting and pottery. However, warfare was an important part of Mycenaean society and unlike Cretan art, much of the Mycenaean pottery,

painting, ivories and inlaid designs on swords, depict soldiers armed with spears and large shields. There are also remains of weapons and armor, including a helmet with boars' tusks, of a type that is mentioned in the Iliad.

From the palace of Pylos and from the latest period at Knossos, are the remains of archives of clay tablets. These are written in the Linear B script, an early form of Greek. Linear B was a development of Linear A, the script used in Minoan Crete. The Mycenaens had adopted Linear A and had developed it to represent Greek.

These texts give a picture of centralized government. Various types of workers are mentioned, including metal-workers, cattle-herders and shepherds, sailors and weavers. Priests, soldiers and rulers also appear. From the archaeological remains and the texts we get a picture of a world of warlike and wealthy kings of independent cities to whom people paid taxes in kind.

All the Mycenaean palaces and towns were destroyed or abandoned by the end of the twelfth century BC. Although there appear to have been invasions, some scholars think that there might have been internal rebellions. However, we do not know what caused the end of this civilization, though we do know it suffered a violent end.

Left. The Lion Gate decorates the impressive gateway that leads to the citadel of 'Golden Mycenae.' Lions were the symbol of kingship.

Above. During the Mycenaean period, warrior kings were buried in 'tholos' tombs such as the one above. This is a reconstruction of the Treasury of Atreus at Mycenae. Atreus was the father of Agamemnon. The doorway leads to a high round chamber which would have held the king's body, along with his weapons and treasure.

Left. A golden death mask from the shaft graves at Mycenae, c. 1570 BC. This mask may have been the death mask of Agamemnon.

THE INDUS VALLEY CIVILIZATION

The Indus Valley

HARAPPA

MOHENJO-DARA

RIVER INDUS

ARABIAN SEA

INDIA

Right. This bust of a bearded man wearing an elaborate shawl comes from the lower part of the town of Mohenjo-Dara. It is thought to represent either a priest or a king and is made of steatite.

People, no doubt, settled in the Indus Valley region because of its fertile conditions. As well as providing excellent conditions for the development of agriculture, the river could supply fish and was used as a means of transport.

Below. A terracotta model of a two-wheeled cart drawn by a bullock. It was found at Harappa, one of the two largest towns of the Indus Valley civilization, and dates from 2500–2000 BC.

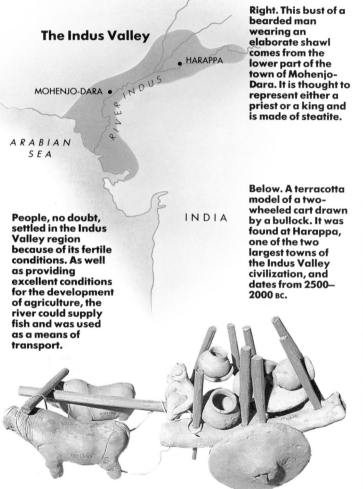

Far to the east of the Aegean, Egyptian and Near Eastern worlds, lay another great center of civilization. It is known as the Indus Valley civilization after the Indus River near to which many of its towns were built.

Covering 500,000 square miles, it was the largest known Bronze Age civilization in the world. More than 150 sites are known and many have been excavated. The two largest are Mohenjo-Dara and Harappa, which were probably the main centers, each with populations of about 30,000 to 40,000 people. As elsewhere, this urban civilization developed from the Neolithic settlements of farming communities, which began around 3500 BC. Gradually, walled towns, trade and specialized crafts emerged, and by 2500 BC, the villages and towns of this vast region were all part of the same civilization.

ORGANIZATION OF THE CITIES Mohenjo-Dara, Harappa and several of the smaller towns had similar plans. The town walls were made of baked brick, and in the center of the town there was a raised area or citadel where the most important buildings were constructed. At Mohenjo-Dara there was a great bath, which may have been used for ritual bathing, rather like the tanks of holy water for bathing in many Indian temples today. Nearby was a building thought to be a granary.

There were no palaces in these cities. The citadel looked over the rest of the town, where there were streets and blocks of houses. The larger houses were arranged around courtyards and had stairs up to a flat roof. Poorer people lived in one-room houses.

Most buildings were of baked brick, which were the same size in all the towns. The streets had drains

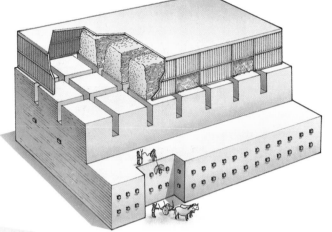

Right. The probable granary, shown here in reconstruction, was situated on the citadel at Mohenjo-Dara on a steep verge. The granary was built of huge timber pieces which were set upon a high brick base, 27 **blocks deep. The criss-cross arrangement of the passages between the blocks insured that the air could circulate beneath it. This was vital to keep the grain fresh. The granary was originally 49.5 yards long and 25.3** **yards wide, but was later extended. A loading platform outside the main building facilitated moving the grain in and out of the stores.**

Above. This is a reconstruction of the Great Bath at Mohenjo-Dara. The building was 13.2 yards long, 7.7 yards wide and 3.3 yards deep. At the north and south ends, brick steps led down to the floor, **with wooden treads which were set in bitumen or asphalt. The bath itself was lined with asphalt in order to make it waterproof.** **The bath was enclosed by verandahs and at the back of three of them were rooms. One of these contained a well, perhaps the source for the water used in the bath. There was also a group of cells with private baths. These are thought to have been used by priests.**

Above. The main blocks of buildings were subdivided by small streets or lanes running parallel to, or at right angles to, the main streets. Some houses were large, such as this one, and consisted of several rooms around a courtyard. There were stairs to **an upper story. Such houses also had a lavatory on the ground or upper floor, a bathroom and a private well. Brick drains were another feature of the Indus Valley towns and they even had their own inspection holes. The house above** **would have belonged to one of the more wealthy townspeople. Poorer people lived in single-room tenements.**

covered in brick, with holes for inspection. Some houses also had bathrooms and lavatories leading to the street drains. Large houses had their own wells. There were also hearths for household fires.

In the lower part of town there were also the workshops of many craftsmen – metalworkers, bead-makers, potters, masons and textile-makers. A standard system of weights and measures was used and many stone weights have been found.

Beautiful *sealstones* carved with animals, were used to seal bales of goods. Some have been found in Iraq, showing that the people of the Indus Valley and Sumer traded with each other. From cuneiform texts, we know that the island of Bahrain, which was called Dilmun, was a center through which this trade passed.

The seals also have hieroglyphic inscriptions on them. These may be the names or titles of merchants but as yet this writing system has not been deciphered. Without written evidence, our knowledge of these people is limited. We still have no idea why the towns were suddenly abandoned and the civilization came to an end about 1700 BC.

LIFE AND DEATH IN ANCIENT CHINA

The civilization of ancient China emerged in the valleys of the Yellow River and Wei River in northern China. Of all the civilizations of the old world, Europe, Asia and Africa, it was the most isolated and owed little to contacts with other regions.

By 6000 BC farmers were working the fertile river valleys. The main crop here was millet and the people reared pigs. These early people made pottery which was beautifully painted.

THE LONGSHAN PERIOD The period from 2500 to 1800 BC is called the *Longshan* period. During this era people lived in towns which were walled for defense. They made metal tools and turned pottery on a wheel. Even then, there were always some people who were far wealthier than others. Archaeological evidence for these developments has been provided by burial practices of the period.

China in the Shang Era

The Shang culture embraced a large area, and rich burials and oracle bones have been unearthed at many of the Shang sites marked on this map. Near Anyang, which was the capital from the 14th to the 11th centuries, are the graves of the last Shang kings, who were buried with their attendants, horses and other animals.

CHINA

YELLOW RIVER

ANYANG
ZHENGZHOU

YELLOW SEA

YANGTZE RIVER

· Major Shang sites
■ Earliest area of Shang influence
□ Area of Shang cultural influence

Left. Examples of the many fine bronze vessels found by archaeologists, dating from the Shang period.

THE SHANG CIVILIZATION The uplands near the fertile valley contained metals which were mined by the people of the early Bronze Age civilization which had developed by about 1800 BC. It is called the *Shang* civilization, from the name of the dynasty of kings who ruled the region.

The Shang capital was moved several times. Zhengzhou was one of the earliest and was founded around 1700 BC. There was a large rammed-earth platform, creating a raised area, on which the palace buildings stood. A wall of 4.2 miles long surrounded this area, and parts of it, about 10 yards high, still survive.

Outside the palace and ceremonial area, were private houses in suburbs, and many workshops. During the Shang period, the skill of the craftsmen advanced dramatically, and beautiful bronze vessels were cast from pottery molds. Among the workshops at Zhengzhou, were pottery kilns and foundries for bronze casting. Several hoards of bronze objects were also found.

Anyang, which became the royal capital in 1400 BC, is the most important Shang site. Here too, was a ceremonial center with palaces, as well as workshops and houses. When the palaces were built, both people and animals were sacrificed and buried in the building foundations and special pits, presumably to make the gods look favorably on the new city. No fewer than 852 people, 35 dogs, 18 sheep, 15 horses, 10 oxen and five chariots, have been found in these pits.

BURIALS AND RELIGION Near to the town were cemeteries, which include the tombs of the last Shang kings. Although many of the tombs were robbed thousands of years ago, the surviving objects give us some idea of the wealth of these rulers.

The kings' servants were sacrificed and buried with the body, as were his horses and dogs. They also buried the kings' chariots, and many bronze and jade objects.

Ancestor worship was an important part of the Chinese people's religion. The ancestors were consulted through the *oracle bones*. These were animal bones or tortoise shells on which questions to the ancestor spirits and the gods were carved. Thousands of oracle bones have been found at Anyang and elsewhere.

The Shang dynasty collapsed in the eleventh century when the Zhou conquered the state. However, many traditions continued, passing into later Chinese civilization.

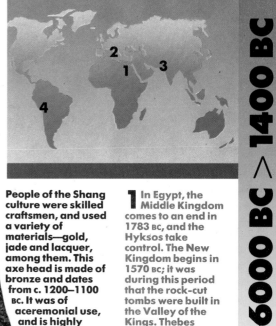

People of the Shang culture were skilled craftsmen, and used a variety of materials—gold, jade and lacquer, among them. This axe head is made of bronze and dates from c. 1200–1100 BC. It was of aceremonial use, and is highly decorated.

1 In Egypt, the Middle Kingdom comes to an end in 1783 BC, and the Hyksos take control. The New Kingdom begins in 1570 BC; it was during this period that the rock-cut tombs were built in the Valley of the Kings. Thebes became the new capital. Tutankhamun was buried in 1337 BC.

2 Palaces are built in Minoan Crete at Knossos, Phaestos and Mallia c. 2000 BC. Cretan hieroglyphic writing begins. The period in Greek history known as 'Mycenaean' begins c. 1550 BC. Mycenaeans take control of Crete c. 1450 BC. The Mycenaean period comes to an end c. 1150 BC.

Right. Neolithic axes made of stone and jade, c. 2500 BC. Several types of stone were used to fashion axes. Jade, however, was the most highly prized and was probably brought a long distance, from Lake Baikal in central Asia.

3 The Indus Valley civilization collapses c. 2000 BC. On the steppes in central Asia, horses are used to pull carts c. 1850 BC, and pastoral nomads herding cattle on horseback appear c. 1400 BC. The bronze industry begins in central Asia c. 1200 BC.

4 The first metalworking begins in Peru c. 1500 BC. The first cities appear in central America c. 1200 BC, inhabited by people of the Olmec culture.

Above and right. Two bronze ritual vessels of the Shang period. The one above was a libation vessel used for pouring offerings of wine, c. 1200–1100 BC. The one to the right was a food vessel. There were many different styles of Shang bronze ritual vessels used to hold either food, wine or water. Their decoration was often very ornate and symbolic.

39

The First People

TIME CHART

	NEAR EAST	AFRICA/EGYPT	EUROPE/GREECE	CHINA/INDIA
	4.5 million BC – 100,000 BC Evolution of Man in Africa Spread of Man from Africa and Palaeolithic Era				
	10,000 BC – 4000 BC Neolithic: Spread of farming/early metalworking				

BC	NEAR EAST	AFRICA/EGYPT	EUROPE/GREECE	CHINA/INDIA
6500			Neolithic farming	
6000	Copper-working in Anatolia	Cattle domesticated		Farming
5000	Irrigation farming		Metalwork in Balkans	
4500				Agriculture
4000		Sail first used in Egypt		
3500	First towns			
3118		Unification of Egypt		
3100	First writing			
2686>2181		Old Kingdom		
2600>2400	Royal Graves of Ur			
2500				Longshan neolithic culture in Taiwan
2372>2255	Akkadian Empire			
2133>1633		Middle Kingdom		
2113>2006	Third Dynasty of Ur			
2000>1900			Greek speaking tribes	
1792>1750	Hammurapi of Babylonia			
1674>1567		Hyksos invaders		
1650>1450			Minoans and Mycenaeans on mainland	
1587>1085		New Kingdom		
1500>1027				Shang dynasty. A feudal empire centred on Anyang
1460>1180	Hittite Empire			
1450			Cretan civilization ends	
1300	Iranians move into Iran			
1200	Raids of Sea Peoples			
1197>1165		Ramesses III defeats Sea Peoples		

40

The Empires of the Ancient World

GREECE

MEDITERRANEAN SEA

PERSIA

CHINA

EGYPT

ARABIA

INDIA

SOUTH CHINA SEA

Athenian Empire
Macedonian Empire
Late Babylonian Empire
Zhou China
Assyrian Empire
Persian Empire

INDIAN OCEAN

Pericles dominated Athenian politics at the height of the Classical Greek period. The extent of Athenian control of the Greek world increased enormously under his direction.

PART TWO

The Great Empires

The thousand years, or *millennium*, before the beginning of our era was the period when iron began to be used in the Near East and when the manufacture of iron goods spread through Europe and Asia. This was a major development; iron is found in many places and it is stronger than copper or bronze for tools and weapons.

Better tools meant improved farming and more food, which resulted in more people. In some places, as the population grew, there was not enough land, so people moved on, seeking new places to live. This is one of the reasons why the Greeks, for instance, started colonies in the Black Sea area and around the southern coast of Italy and elsewhere. It is also the reason for the various movements of people on the fringes of the civilized world.

Iron also meant that armies were better equipped.

The need for more land was sometimes backed by armed force, and in time some countries took control of others and formed *empires*. The Assyrians did this, so did the Babylonians and later, the Persians.

There were other inventions that changed life. The development of a keel on ships meant that sailors could take their vessels into the open sea and travel further. The alphabet made writing simpler and much easier to learn, so writing became increasingly widespread and more information was written down. This means among other things, that there is far more written evidence from which historians can gather facts, including accounts of events by Greek historians. From these, and from poetry, plays and other works, we have far more detail about what life was like for these people than for those who lived earlier.

Population Movements
THE PHILISTINES AND ISRAELITES

Lands of the Middle East c. 900 BC

This map shows the lands and major cities of the Middle East around 900 BC. Jerusalem had been carefully selected by David as his new capital. It was strategically placed and was easily defendable, as it stood among rugged hills. As David's capital it served three purposes. It was the seat of the royal house of David; the center of government for all Israel; and a religious capital— the site of 'Yahweh's' future temple.

Phoenicia
Israel
Philistia
Judah

In about 1200 BC there were great upheavals in the lands of the eastern Mediterranean Sea. The Hittite empire vanished suddenly and cities of the Levant were laid waste.

THE SEA PEOPLE It is generally thought that these disturbances were caused by groups of roving marauders called 'the Sea People.' It is possible that the Sea People were linked to the destruction and abandonment of the Mycenaean centers of the Aegean and Troy, but nothing is known for certain.

From Egyptian accounts we know that the Sea People attacked Egypt but were defeated. Pharaoh Ramesses III had his victory recorded: *The foreign countries made a plot in their islands . . . no land could stand before their arms, beginning with Khatti (the Hittites) . . . They came, onwards to Egypt . . . as for those who reached my boundary . . . their hearts and their souls are finished unto eternity– those who entered unto the river mouths were confined . . . butchered and their corpses hacked up.*

Some settled on Egypt's borders and later became mercenaries for the Pharaoh. Others, the Peleset, settled in southern Canaan around Gaza. Known as the Philistines, they gave their name to Palestine.

Events in the century before the first *millenium* BC (one thousand years), are not very clear and there is a break in the archaeological record. What is known, is that by 1000 BC there were several new groups of people living in the Near East. Also, the great powers such as Egypt and Babylonia had grown weaker.

THE CULTURE OF THE ISRAELITES Because there was no powerful state in control, groups of migrating nomads were able to settle in Syria and Palestine. Among them were the Israelites, the group whom we know most about.

The Israelites believed in the power of their god 'Yahweh' above all others. They despised other gods and in time they believed that no other god existed. From the eighth century BC, they wrote down their history and laws. These books were preserved, some as part of the Christian Old Testament. *Monotheism*, the belief in one god, was of great importance, because it was from this tradition that both Christianity and Islam were to come.

Apart from religion, their lives were no different from other people in this region. They were farmers living in villages and small, walled towns. They were also sturdy fighters and after arriving in Canaan, had fought the Philistines and the Canaanites.

The Israelites' greatest period was during the reigns of David and Solomon, from 1000 – 926 BC when there was one kingdom with its capital Jerusalem in Judah. David had captured and refortified the city and Solomon had a splendid temple and palace built here by Phoenician craftsmen.

In 926 BC the kingdom was divided into Israel (north) and Judah (south). King Omri of Israel built himself a new capital at Samaria which had a beautiful palace. Later, Israel became an Assyrian province, and in 597 BC the Babylonians took Jerusalem, and in the process the king and his nobles were exiled to Babylon.

Left. Human-shaped or anthropomorphic coffins were used by the Philistines. This sarcophagus lid dates from the 12th century BC. It is made of clay and is typical of the styles made during this period.

Above. A household shrine of the Israelite period, but probably Philistine. Such shrines were widely used among the people of this region. The voluted columns resemble the proto-Ionic columns used on some buildings of this period.

1 1085 BC marked the end of the New Kingdom in Egypt. The country was effectively divided with Upper Egypt controlled from Thebes, and Lower Egypt under the control of competing dynasts, including descendants of Libyan chiefs. The Kingdom of Kush (Nubia) was founded in 900 BC. This date also marked the beginning of the Nok culture of Nigeria.

2 By 1000 BC, hillforts were in use in western Europe, and iron was widely in use in the Aegean and central Europe. The period known as the 'Dark Ages' in Greece ended in 900 BC. In Italy, the settlement of Rome begins c. 850 BC.

3 In China, the Zhou Dynasty replaced the Shang Dynasty in 1027 BC. Bronze-working spreads from China to Korea.

4 Larger communities start to appear in the central and south Andes of South America c. 1000 BC. At the same period in North America, the Indians of the Adena culture in the east begin the practice of richly furnishing their burials. Grave goods such as bracelets, rings, beads, tobacco pipes and polished stone tools were commonly placed with the corpse under the burial mound.

5 Around 1000 BC long distance trade networks for raw materials develop. In the southeast of Australia, villages with round stone houses appear.

Solomon's Temple

The temple built by Solomon was finished in the eleventh year of his reign. It is not possible to know how it looked exactly, though some idea can be gained from the description in the Bible, and from what is known about Canaan art in this period.

The walls were of stone blocks and were plain on the outside, but covered on the inside with cedar wood and carved figures of winged creatures, palm trees and rosettes.

Two large bronze pillars stood either side of the gold-inlaid, olivewood doors.

There were also bronze basins on ornamental wheeled pedestals for washing burnt offerings. At the back of the interior were steps leading to the 'Holy of Holies' where stood the ark of the covenant containing the 10 commandment written on stone tablets.

THE PHOENICIANS

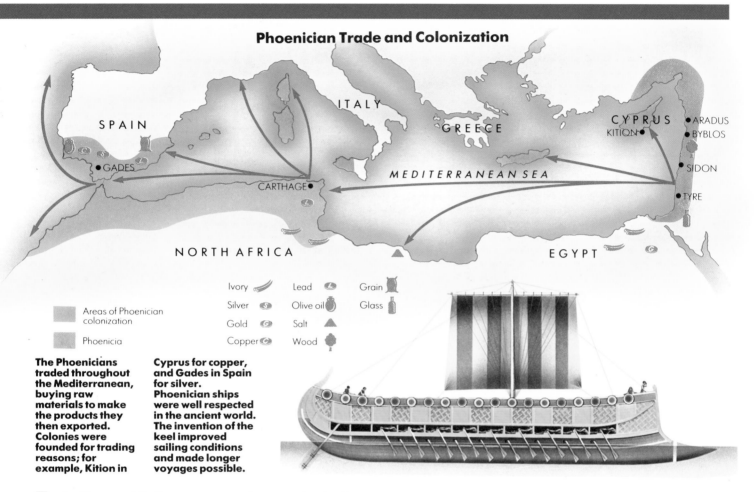

Phoenician Trade and Colonization

SPAIN
ITALY
GREECE
CYPRUS • ARADUS
KITION • • BYBLOS
• SIDON
• TYRE
• GADES
CARTHAGE •
MEDITERRANEAN SEA
NORTH AFRICA
EGYPT

Ivory   Lead   Grain

Silver   Olive oil   Glass

Gold   Salt

Copper   Wood

Areas of Phoenician colonization

Phoenicia

The Phoenicians traded throughout the Mediterranean, buying raw materials to make the products they then exported. Colonies were founded for trading reasons; for example, Kition in Cyprus for copper, and Gades in Spain for silver. Phoenician ships were well respected in the ancient world. The invention of the keel improved sailing conditions and made longer voyages possible.

In the Eastern Mediterranean, ancient peoples had long been linked by sea-borne trade. In 2000 BC Egyptian and Minoan ships sailed between Egypt, the Levant and Greece. Later, the Mycenaeans took to the sea, trading wine, honey, fine oils, pottery and metals.

This trade was brought to an end when the Sea People laid waste the lands of the eastern Mediterranean. As on land, so on the sea, there was no longer one great power. Thus the cities of the Levant and Syrian coast were able to take control of the seaborne trade.

The people of these cities were the Phoenicians known to the Greeks as 'Phoinikes' the purple men. They were perhaps called this because of the famous Tyrian purple dye with which they dyed the cloth that they exported.

The Phoenicians called themselves 'Kinahu' or 'Canaanites,' after the name of the whole region, although they lived on the narrow coastal strip which

today forms Israel and Lebanon. Here, cedar and fir trees grew on the mountains that divided the coast from the inland regions. From this timber the Phoenicians built themselves sturdy ships.

PHOENICIAN SOCIETY AND TRADE The Phoenician cities were each independent states, although sometimes they would form alliances with each other. The most important cities were Tyre, Sidon, Byblos and Aradus.

High stone walls and towers protected the towns. These were sometimes built on islands for further protection, or on land jutting out to the sea. The invention of lime mortar for water cisterns meant that cities like Tyre could be situated on islands where there was no water. The houses were double storied with balconies.

As early as 3000 BC cedars of Lebanon were exported to Egypt, where there was little good timber. Apart from wood and dyed fabrics, the Phoenicians

Above. The Phoenicians were famous for their skill with ivory. Elephants were extinct in Syria by 1000 BC, so stocks had to be imported from India or Africa. This piece depicts a sphinx and dates from the ninth century BC.

Right. Glassmaking developed in the second millenium BC. From about 600 BC the Phoenicians produced glass vessels that were almost colorless. They also produced colored glass such as this bottle shown here. Colored glass was made by adding pigments during the glassmaking process.

Above. 'The woman at the window' was a popular subject for ivory makers. She is thought to represent the sacred prostitute of the cult of Ashtart.

The woman is dressed in an Egyptian wig and clothing. This ivory dates from the ninth/eighth century BC.

Tyrian Purple

Tyrian purple was a highly prized dye. It was made from a gland found in the 'murex' — an offshore mollusk, or shellfish. The gland secretion was boiled up with various fixatives, and the intensity of the color depended on the length of time the fabric was treated.

Colors could range from pink to deep purple — the famed 'Royal Purple of Tyre.' In antiquity, purple was the color of royalty.

Left. This ivory depicts a lioness attacking a slave in a thicket of lotus and papyrus. It is one of a pair which were probably originally used as furniture panels on a throne or elaborate chair. The subject matter was originally Egyptian, symbolizing Egypt defeating the foreigner, but became a Phoenician decorative theme.

The Phoenician Alphabet

H   K   L   M   N   Q

The alphabet was first developed in the Middle East about 1600 BC. The earliest known alphabet is called the North Semitic. Two other alphabets stemmed from it: the Aramaic and the Canaanite.

It was from the Canaanite that the Phoenicians developed their alphabet. Almost all present-day alphabets are derived from the Phoenician. Their alphabet consisted entirely of

consonants, and it was the Greeks who added vowels at a later date. The Romans gave it the form that we use today.

traded glass and ivory carvings. When Omri of Israel built his palace at Samaria it was decorated with Phoenician ivory carving. They were also famous for their stone carving and Phoenician craftsmen built Solomon's temple at Jerusalem. The Phoenicians also acted as middlemen in trade – that is buying and selling goods from elsewhere, that they had not produced.

Metal ores were very important as they were used for weapons, tools and jewelry. Copper came from Cyprus, where the Phoenicians founded a colony. They also discovered rich deposits of silver in Spain where they founded a colony at Gades, modern Cadiz.

In 814 BC Carthage in North African was founded by the city of Tyre. At first it was only a staging post on the long journey to Spain, but it grew to be a great city.

The greatest legacy of the Phoenicians was their alphabetic writing system. This was adopted by the Greeks with whom they competed as traders. From the Greeks it has gradually passed down in time to us.

THE SCYTHIANS – NOMADS OF THE STEPPES

The Scythians were nomadic people of the *steppes*, the enormous belt of grassland stretching across Asia from Manchuria to Russia. Broken in parts by the desert, the steppes border forest to the north and desert and dry regions to the south.

Unlike the farmers and town-dwellers of the settled lands, the Scythians lived by stock-breeding and some hunting. They raised herds of sheep, cattle and horses. They practiced *transhumance*, which means moving their herds from summer pasture on higher ground, to winter pasture on lower ground each year.

As they were on the move twice a year, the horse and wagon were very important for carrying the people and their belongings, all of which were portable.

MOVING ON

In the eighth century BC, they were driven westward, probably by the activities of a stronger group than themselves. As they moved across this vast area, they came into contact, and often conflict, with the civilized lands to the south.

Some moved into south Russia, where they came into contact with the Greeks of the Black Sea towns. The Greek writer Herodotus wrote an account of them in his history.

Those who settled in northern Iran fought the Medes, while their presence in Armenia brought about the downfall of Urartu. Many settled for a long period in Anatolia.

Other groups settled east of the Caspian Sea, creating problems for the Persians. A related group, called the Cimmerians, fought with the Medes and Babylonians against Assyria.

SWIFT WARRIORS

The picture given by the Chinese and Greek accounts, is of fierce and highly mobile warriors, almost one with their small swift horses. They fought on horseback, using the bow and arrow. According to one account, they scalped their enemies and kept the hair as a trophy.

LEARNING ABOUT THE PEOPLE

Once again, we can learn much about these people from their graves. These have been found in southern Russia, as well as northern Mongolia, south of Lake Baikal and in the Altai Mountains. Because they were nomadic, there are no remains of towns to investigate. The other source of evidence comes from the written records of the people who came into contact with them, particularly the Chinese in the east and the Greeks in the west.

Some of their tombs have been very well preserved by ice which effectively sealed the tombs. Rich hangings, carpets, cushions and saddlecloths with lovely designs have been found in the tombs, as well as beautiful silks. The bodies of the dead were covered with elaborate tatoos.

When a chief died, his wife and servants were killed and buried with him, as were his horses. Many very beautiful golden objects have been found in Scythian burials, which give an idea of their wealth.

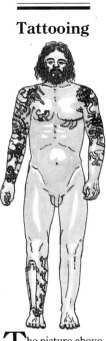

Tattooing

Above. This magnificent gold comb from a grave of the burial mound, or 'kungan,' at Solocha, was made in the late fifth/early fourth century BC. The handle shows details of Scythians in battle.

Right. Details from the frieze of figures on the amphora from the Čertomlyk 'kungan' in the CIS. The horses are being trained and one is having its legs hobbled before being put to pasture.

The picture above shows the tattooing on a body found at the second 'kungan' at Pazyryk in the CIS. Bronze mirrors were also found in the tomb, which indicates that the Scythians cared about their appearance.

According to the Greek historian, Herodotus, tattooing was the mark of high birth, and the lack of it a mark of low birth. Often the designs were carefully arranged so that the person was a 'living' work of art.

Scythian Burials

When dead, the Scythians were placed in graves within 'kungans,' or burial mounds. Some were 'catacomb'-type tombs hollowed out of the ground as in the diagram above. Scythian chiefs and warriors were buried with their horses and carts. Their retainers and wives were also buried with them. Many very wealthy Scythians were buried with huge quantities of grave goods of gold and silver.

Above. The burial chamber of a rich Scythian with all his riches alongside.

Right. Two burial chambers showing horses buried with their owners.

Mesopotamian Empires
THE ASSYRIAN EMPIRE

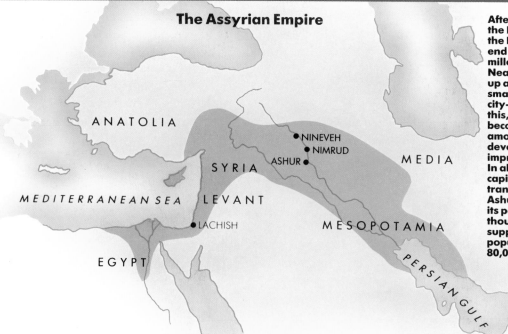

The Assyrian Empire

ANATOLIA

NINEVEH
NIMRUD
ASHUR

SYRIA

MEDIA

MEDITERRANEAN SEA LEVANT

LACHISH

MESOPOTAMIA

EGYPT

PERSIAN GULF

After the decline of the Egyptians and the Hittites at the end of the second millennium BC, the Near East was split up among many small kingdoms and city-states. Out of this, Assyria rose to become dominant among them, and to develop a large and impressive empire. In about 880 BC the capital was transferred from Ashur to Nimrud. At its peak, Nimrud is thought to have supported a population of 80,000. Later Nineveh became the capital. All the capitals were based around a citadel which housed temples and palaces. These buildings were elaborately and richly furnished and decorated. The Assyrians managed to maintain and increase the limit of the empire through relentless military conquest.

The Assyrians were the first people to unite most of the Near East under imperial control. Both the Hittites and Egyptians had expanded their territories and controlled foreign subjects by telling their rulers what to do.

Where the Assyrian Empire differs from these earlier empires is that its conquests and the extent of its power were on a much wider scale. The heartland of Assyria was situated in northern Mesopotamia. The climate of this region was different to that of the south, with enough rain to grow plenty of crops for an expanding city.

In the ninth century BC, the Assyrians began to expand their territory under a series of strong kings. At first they took control of northern Syria from the Armaeans. Then they battled with Urartu to the north, and later with the Egyptians and Babylonians. The Empire expanded until Assyria controlled much of the area from the Persian Gulf to Egypt.

To control this Empire, a system of provincial administration was set up. All provinces were obliged to offer tribute. A governor who was responsible for tax collection ruled each province from his palace in the provincial capital. These establishments were much smaller but similar to the royal palaces in Nimrud and Nineveh.

CAPITALS OF THE EMPIRE The earliest capital had been Ashur, where the kings were always buried. Ashurnasirpal II moved his capital to Nimrud. He enlisted workmen from all over his Empire to build a great palace there. When the building was finished, he gave a banquet. An inscription has survived which describes the banquet: there were 70,000 guests and they drank 10,000 bottles of wine and ate 14,000 sheep and many other things. Later Nineveh became the royal center, where Sennacherib (704–681 BC) built his 'palace without rival.' This had beautiful gardens, watered by streams led from the river.

THE ARMY The Assyrian army was well organized. At first, the soldiers were peasants and were positioned mainly in the capital alone. But as the Empire grew, there were *detachments* of soldiers enlisted from the provinces as well.

Garrisons were stationed in the provinces to maintain Assyrian control. Good roads and grain storage facilities were built so that messengers could move quickly and get fresh horses and food supplies.

Internal strife and external pressure, brought about by rebellions of the member states of the Empire, gradually weakened Assyria. In 612 Nineveh fell to the Medes and Babylonians and by 609 the Empire had fallen.

The Siege of Lachish

The siege of Lachish was the final act in Sennacherib's campaign to take control of Judah. Although documentary evidence about the siege is not complete, reliefs from Sennacherib's palace at Nineveh (see right) provide a rich record of events and military technology used.

The Assyrian army included archers, slingmen and spearmen. Archers were the main arm of the military unit, and soldiers with large shields were used to protect the archers when under fire. The Assyrians also used siege engines and battering rams.

Left. This relief from the palace at Nineveh, depicts part of Sennacherib's siege of the Israelite city of Lachish. A siege engine can be seen battering the walls of the city, and prisoners are coming from the gate.

Below. An aerial view of the ancient city of Lachish. Excavations at the site have yielded some of the actual stones thrown by the stoneslingers during the siege of the city in 701 BC.

Right. A scene from the siege of Lachish. Israelite captives are being flayed alive on stakes outside the city. This relief is from the palace at Nineveh and is dated c. 700 BC.

1 The earliest archaeological evidence points to the Phoenician founding of Carthage in 750 BC. In 600 BC the Nubian capital moves to Meroë. Northern Africa becomes a major ironworking center.

2 From 900–750 BC the city-states begin to emerge in Greece, and from 800 BC in central Italy the Etruscan city-states begin to develop. The first Olympic Games are held in Greece in 776 BC. The first Greek alphabet inscription, adapted from the Phoenician alphabet, is dated to 750 BC. The Etruscan script is developed from Greek c. 690 BC. Around 600 BC the first Greek coins are used. During this period Rome develops into a town and the Latin script is first used.

3 Cities in the Ganges valley in India emerge c. 800 BC and rice cultivation begins. The Eastern Zhou hold power in China from 770 BC, and the capital is moved to Luoyang. Elephants are used for warfare in India from c. 600 BC.

4 The first writing in the Americas develops among the Zapotecs of Mexico c. 800 BC.

Left. This is a statue of King Ashurnasirpal II. He was the great king who defeated many of the Armaean states in the upper Euphrates area, and extended the boundaries to the great bend of that river. He moved the capital from Ashur to Nimrud, where he built a great palace. This statue comes from Nimrud and shows him holding the mace of kingship.

THE LATE BABYLONIAN EMPIRE

After the fall of the Assyrian Empire, the ancient city of Babylon became the center of an empire which reached to the borders of Egypt.

THE CREATION OF AN EMPIRE Nabopolassar, the first of the *Neo-Babylonian* rulers, had defeated Assyria with the help of the Medes at Nineveh in 612. Then he and his son, Nebuchadrezzar II, took control of the Assyrian provinces in the west.

Above. Detail of the mythical 'Marduk' that once adorned the Ishtar Gate of Babylon.

Below. Under Nebuchadrezzar, Babylon was splendidly rebuilt and extended. In the center stood the great ziggurat and the Temple of Marduk.

Within a few years Nebuchadrezzar had created a great empire, which included Judah. To maintain control of Judah, the Jewish king and nobles of Jerusalem were taken into captivity and were exiled to Babylon.

The provinces were ruled by Babylonian governors, although some were left in the care of local rulers who were loyal to Babylon. The temples had to give one tenth of their income (from temple lands) to the king. They resented this and it is possible that the dissatisfaction of the priests later resulted in their support of King Cyrus of Persia, who took the city without a battle in 539 BC.

The fall of Babylon is dramatically told in the Biblical story of 'Balshazzar's feast' where Daniel is called to interpret the writing on the wall. Although it is a story and not an historical incident, we know from cuneiform texts that Balshazzar was in fact the Crown Prince, and he died fighting the Persians outside Babylon.

THE GREAT CITY OF BABYLON Babylon was so famous that the Greek historian Herodotus wrote a detailed description of the city. Most of the building was done by Nabopolassar who had defeated the Assyrians, and his son Nebuchadrezzar. They made Babylon far more splendid than it had formerly been.

The Late Babylonian Empire

Key Dates

729 BC	Tiglathpileser becomes king of Babylon
689 BC	Sennacherib of Assyria destroyed Babylon
625–605 BC	Nabopolassar led fight against Assyrians with Persian support
605–562 BC	Nebuchadrezzar ruled Babylon
539 BC	Babylon captured by the Persians.

Above. This is a reconstruction of the gateway of Marduk. Marduk was the city god who became prominent in the 17th century BC. He is represented in the form of a dragon.

Huge walls surrounded the city and the inner ones were so wide that a chariot with four horses could travel along them. There were several city gates, each named after one of the gods. The goddess of love and war was *Ishtar*, and from the great *Ishtar Gate* a long processional way led to the temples and palaces.

Both the gate and the sacred way were covered with brilliant blue glazed tiles on which were raised reliefs of lions, bulls and dragons. Each animal was linked to a god: the lion to Ishtar; the bull to Adad, god of the sky and weather; and the dragon to Marduk, the god of the city.

Within the city were numerous temples and palaces. The great temple of Marduk stood next to the *ziggurat* or temple tower. Near the river was the palace, which was also beautifully decorated with glazed tiles. Here were the famous Hanging Gardens that stood on man-made terraces. The garden was originally created for a Median princess who missed the trees and cooler weather of her homeland. The gardens are one of the Seven Wonders of the Ancient World.

As the city grew it extended to the other side of the river. There were numerous houses and shops for the large population.

Nowadays, all that remains are the mud brick foundations, for later the river shifted its course, causing Babylon to be abandoned.

The Persian Empire
IRAN AND THE RISE OF PERSIA

The Beginnings of the Persian Empire

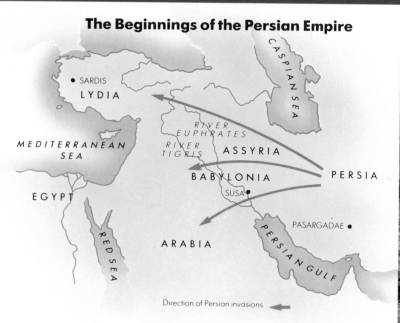

Direction of Persian invasions

From their homeland the Persians spread throughout the Near East to eventually form the largest empire the world had ever seen until then. (For the full extent of the Empire, see map on page 55.) Their earliest conquests included Lydia, Assyria and Babylon.

Iran, which lies to the east of the Mesopotamian valley was the homeland of the Medes and Persians. It is very different from the lands between the Tigris and the Euphrates Rivers. Parts are desert, although the valleys between the mountains are fertile.

The southwest of the country is part of the Mesopotamian plain and here, as in Sumer, were some of the earliest cities in the world. This was the kingdom of *Elam*, and these people had a pictographic script, which cannot yet be read, so little is known of their history.

MEDES AND PERSIANS Because it can be easily reached from Central Asia, many nomads came to Iran, including the Iranians, an *Indo-European* people. They came from the steppes in about 1300 BC, and spread throughout the land. Among those who settled in the west were the Medes and Persians. Because much time was spent on horseback, the Medes wore trousers and felt hats similar to those of other nomads in Asia.

Gradually these people became powerful and in

Above. A view of the acropolis at Sardis. The acropolis was fortified during the Lydian period, but during construction, one small area where there was a narrow steep drop was left unfortified. This proved to be the Lydians' undoing during the Persian attack. It was through this gap that a Persian soldier climbed to open the city gates for the army.

Left. Strip of gold of unknown purpose. The style is of Scythian or Russian influence c. 800–700 BC. Above. Part of a necklace of gold and pearl beads from Pasargadae in Iran. Very few pearls have survived from an early date. These pearls probably came from the Persian Gulf.

Croesus, the Last King of Lydia

According to legend, Croesus, the defeated Lydian king, was saved by Apollo from execution at the last minute by Cyrus.

Herodotus, the Greek historian, tells us that Cyrus had already changed his mind about the execution, and demanded that the fire that had been lit under Croesus be put out.

The flames, however, had already taken hold. Croesus then called upon Apollo to save him. At this point, clouds gathered and a storm broke out with such violent rain that the fire was extinguished. The illustration on this amphora shows the pyre being lit.

The tholos at Delphi was built c. 400 BC in the sanctuary of Athena below the oracular shrine. By the beginning of the seventh century BC, the practice had begun of oriental kings making dedications at Delphi to win the favor of Apollo. Even before the time of Croesus the Phrygian king, Midas, and an earlier Lydian king, Gyges, are reported to have made offerings to the Delphic oracle. The offerings of Croesus however totally eclipsed all former dedications. Croesus had sent a lion made of pure gold weighing a quarter of a ton, and vessels of gold and silver. This generosity of Croesus' was made with a view to gaining favorable oracular responses. The responses of the oracle were a serious matter in ancient Greece, and the oracle would be consulted on such important issues as whether to go to war with another state.

612 BC the Medes helped the Babylonians to defeat Assyria. The Persian king, Cyrus the Great, whose mother was a Mede, united the Medes and Persians. He then began the conquests that made the Persian Empire the largest of the ancient empires. First he defeated Lydia which was in Anatolia. Lydia was ruled by the immensely wealthy king, Croesus from his capital at Sardis. The Lydians were the first people to use coins – that is, a standard weight of metal guaranteed by the state. Lydia's wealth came from the gold of the Pactolus river which flowed through Sardis.

THE ORACLES Before the conflict with Cyrus, Croesus asked for advice from the Delphic oracle. An oracle was a kind of prophecy that told what would happen. These prophecies were made by priests or priestesses attached to sacred places like Delphi, situated in Greece, which was home to the oracle of the Greek god Apollo. Because the Lydians were neighbors of the Greeks, and in general on good terms, they also consulted Greek oracles.

Sometimes the priests were bribed to give helpful oracles. Often the oracles were not clear and could be interpreted in various ways – as happened to Croesus. He was told somewhat confusingly, that if he crossed the Halys River a great empire would fall. Taking this to mean Cyrus' empire, Croesus crossed the Halys and was himself defeated. Cyrus is said to have spared Croesus' life.

The conquest of Lydia meant that Cyrus now controlled the Greek cities of the coast of Asia Minor. He returned to Persia and then captured Babylon in 539 BC. He took the Babylonian throne, not as a conqueror, but ruling according to local customs. This was very important as it meant that he gained the support of many Babylonians and their former subjects. He allowed the Jews to return to Jerusalem in 537 BC and to rebuild their temple there.

By the time of his death in 530 BC, Cyrus had laid the foundations of the Persian Empire.

DARIUS I AND THE EMPIRE

The remains of the Palace of Darius at Persepolis. The Palace overlooked the plain and rose very high. The door and window frames of polished dark stone now stand alone, as the mud brick walls have perished.

Cambyses, the son of Cyrus, conquered Egypt in 526 BC, as his father had planned to do. The Persian Empire now reached from the Indus River to the Nile.

THE ORGANIZATION OF THE EMPIRE The next ruler was Darius I who reorganized the empire, after he had put down the rebellions against his taking of the throne. He created *Satrapies*, or provinces, which were ruled by loyal Persians. There were 20 Satrapies in total, each ruled by a Persian noble or member of the royal family. A separate official, in charge of the army, collected the tribute from each province. This could be paid in many ways: in gold, silver, animals, slaves, incense from Arabia, ivory from Ethiopia or even camels from Bactria.

A system of roads was built, to make travel throughout the Empire easier. On the Royal Road from Susa in Persia to Ephesus in Anatolia, a royal courier could travel the 1,620 miles in a week. Fresh horses were kept at stables along the way.

Darius also had a canal cut from the Red Sea to the

The Behistun Relief

In 522 BC Darius I had a large inscription placed 120 metres high on the great rock of Behistun. The king stands with his foot on the would-be usurper Gaumata. Two attendants are behind him and facing him are the nine rebel kings. The cuneiform inscription is in three languages, old Persian, Akkadian and Elamite.

It was the copying and deciphering of the old Persian version, that led to the decipherment of cuneiform.

Nile, so that ships could travel from the Indian Ocean to the Mediterranean in a much quicker time. He also built an entire fleet.

WAR WITH THE SCYTHIANS In 512 BC Darius set out to the Black Sea area to fight against the Scythians. His aim was to stop them sending timber to the Greeks for their ships. He crossed the River Danube, but the Scythians had burned the crops, so he could get no supplies for his

Right. Many of the decorations on the buildings at Persepolis were very elaborate. Though this carving now lies in the sand, it was once the capital of a column. The carving shows a double-headed eagle.

Left. This is a relief from the Treasury at Persepolis showing King Darius receiving homage from Median and Persian nobles.

Above. A reconstruction of the Apadana, or audience hall, at the Palace. The Apadana had 36 interior columns, and leading off it were three porticoes, each with 12 columns. It was probably hung with tapestries inside, as shown here. The purpose of the buildings at Persepolis is not known, for there seem to be no places where people could actually have lived. It would appear that it served only as a ceremonial center. When in attendance, the court and visitors would have stayed in specially erected tents.

The Persian Empire

THRACE

ANATOLIA

EPHESUS

MEDITERRANEAN SEA

BACTRIA

PERSIA
SUSA • PASARGADAE
• PERSEPOLIS

EGYPT

RED SEA

The Persian Empire depended on good communications. Greek writers refer to the presence of the Royal Road from Susa to Ephesus and we can map its probable route. But little trace is left of the Road today.

army. However, he had managed to add Thrace to his empire, which meant that he now controlled the narrow straits, the Dardanelles, between Asia and Europe.

PERSIAN PALACES Darius treated his subject people fairly. Many foreign craftsmen worked at the palaces he built at Susa and Persepolis. He moved his capital to Susa, which was warmer in winter than the old capital Pasargadae. In gratitude to the army for its support, he had his bodyguard, the 'Ten Thousand Immortals,' portrayed on the palace walls at Susa.

At Persepolis the king celebrated the Persian New Year festival. The palace was built on a raised terrace of 33 acres. On the terrace were two reception halls. Darius began the great 'Apadana' of 66 yards square, but it was finished by his son, Xerxes. Its 36 columns were made of cedarwood. The second hall, 77 yards square, was built by Xerxes.

It was here that Alexander the Great held a feast before burning down the palace.

THE FALL OF THE PERSIAN EMPIRE

The death of Darius I in 486 BC marked the end of the greatest days of the Empire. Unfortunately, much of what is known of events after Darius I, comes from the Greeks, and may not be fair to the Persians, as there was always strong rivalry and hostilities between the Greeks and Persians.

In 480 BC Xerxes led an army of 70,000 against the Greeks across the Dardanelles on a bridge of boats. Although he was successful at first, the war ended in failure.

THE START OF THE DECLINE From the late fifth century BC, there was strife and rebellion within the Persian Empire. Civil war broke out in the fourth century, and from late in this century, several rulers were murdered. Court intrigues had long been a problem for the Achaemenid kings. Darius III, the last ruler of the Empire, was placed on the throne in 336 BC by the manipulations of the eunuch Bagoas.

Five years later the Empire was lost to Alexander the Great, and the once mighty Persian Empire was now to become part of the new Hellenistic world.

The Greeks regarded the Persians as a people who had become decadent and luxury-loving since the great days of Cyrus. The many beautiful objects of gold and silver made by their craftsmen are indeed luxurious and reflect the great wealth of the Persian king and his satraps and nobles.

Key Dates of the Persian Empire

550 BC	Cyrus becomes king of the Medes and Persians.
530 BC	Death of Cyrus and accession of Cambyses II.
522–520 BC	Accession of Darius and internal rebellion.
490 BC	Invasion of Greece. Persians defeated at Marathon.
480–479 BC	Persians defeated by Greeks at Thermopylae, Salamis and Plataea.
336–330 BC	Rise of Alexander and defeat of Persia. Persepolis burned.

A detail from the 'Alexander Sarcophagus' from the Royal Cemetery at Sidon, c. fourth century BC. A Greek cavalryman is shown attacking a Persian. The Persians are depicted wearing trousers and Persian headdress.

The Oxus Treasure

Right. A hollow fish beaten from flat gold sheet. It might have been used as a flask or bottle. It dates from the sixth century BC.

Above. Gold jug with a lion-headed handle. The lion is represented as biting the rim of the fluted body. It dates from the fifth century BC.
Below. A shallow gold bowl, c. sixth century BC. It depicts pairs of lions on their hind legs with their forearms outstretched.

Right. Gold armlet with winged-horned griffin finials, originally inlaid with glass and colored stones. It dates from the fifth/fourth centuries BC.

123919

The Oxus Treasure contains some 170 items of gold and silver dating from the sixth-fourth centuries BC. It is said to have been found on the banks of the Oxus River (near the borders of modern Afghanistan and the CIS) in 1877.

The origins of the treasure are not known, nor is it known who concealed it or why. Although most pieces date from the Hellenistic period, some are of Achaemenid date or even earlier, and the objects show a wide range of styles.

We are fortunate to have the treasure since three years after it was found, it was nearly lost when bandits attacked merchant ships. The robbers were caught and the treasure reclaimed, although some pieces had already been cut up in preparation for melting down.

The Greek World
EARLY GREECE

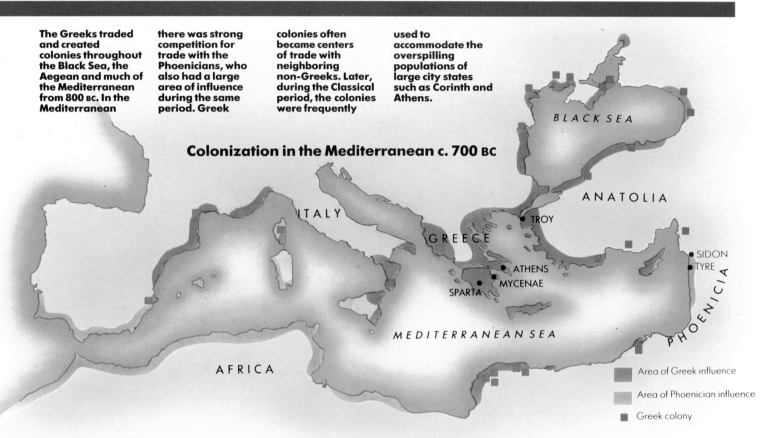

The Greeks traded and created colonies throughout the Black Sea, the Aegean and much of the Mediterranean from 800 BC. In the Mediterranean there was strong competition for trade with the Phoenicians, who also had a large area of influence during the same period. Greek colonies often became centers of trade with neighboring non-Greeks. Later, during the Classical period, the colonies were frequently used to accommodate the overspilling populations of large city states such as Corinth and Athens.

Colonization in the Mediterranean c. 700 BC

ITALY

BLACK SEA

ANATOLIA

GREECE

TROY

ATHENS
MYCENAE
SPARTA

SIDON
TYRE

PHOENICIA

MEDITERRANEAN SEA

AFRICA

Area of Greek influence

Area of Phoenician influence

Greek colony

After the collapse of the Mycenaean world, around 1200 BC, a new group of people came into Greece. They are known as the Dorians and they spoke a dialect of Greek.

Little is known about the period up to the ninth century, and for this reason it is called the 'Dark Age.' The country was very poor and the population had declined, perhaps to as little as a tenth of what it had been in Mycenaean times. From about 1000 BC, poverty led people to migrate from the mainland to the coast of Asia Minor and the Aegean islands, looking for a better life.

EPIC POETRY Many skills had been lost, in particular people no longer wrote things down until the society eventually became illiterate. Nevertheless, the origins of two of the world's greatest poems date back to this period. Although the *Iliad* and the *Odyssey* were written by Homer some time in the mid-eighth century, they are *epic poems* that had been passed down orally through the centuries.

The poems contain references to many *artifacts* of

the Mycenaean world, now known to us from archaeological finds – boars' tusk helmets, gold drinking cups and enormous shields. 'Golden Mycenae' is a world of riches long gone, but still celebrated in the epic poems of Homer.

The *Iliad* tells of the warriors who attacked Troy (see page 32). The *Odyssey* recounts the warrior Odysseus' journey home to the island of *Ithaca* after the ten-year seige of Troy. His journey is long and fraught with dangerous adventures until he is finally reunited with his faithful wife, Penelope. Although there are elements of the Mycenaean age, the world of Odysseus also reflects a picture of the late Dark Ages.

PROSPERITY RETURNS In about 900 BC the Greeks began to trade with the Near Eastern countries of the Mediterranean and with Italy. Life gradually became more prosperous and the population began to increase. The Near Eastern contact influenced artistic design in both pottery and metalwork. The Greeks also acquired an alphabet, adapted from that of the Phoenicians, which brought literacy back to Greece.

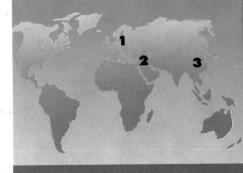

Below. Odysseus and his men blinding Polyphemus, the one-eyed monster known as the Cyclops.

1 The iron industry becomes established in the Aegean and central Europe c. 1000 BC, and spreads to Britain c. 750 BC. The Celtic culture emerges north and east of the Alps c. 800 BC, and this marks the first phase of the Celtic Iron Age.

2 The Hittite Empire collapses c. 1200 BC. The Assyrian Empire is formed c. 950 BC and it goes on to unite almost all of the Near East.

3 The Zhou Dynasty begins in China in 1027 BC, replacing the Shang. This marked the beginning of the Western Zhou period. The beginning of the Eastern Zhou period in China starts in 770 BC, and the capital is moved to Loyang.

Above. This vase painting depicts Odysseus bound to the ship's mast so that he would not succumb to the seductive voices of the sirens.

Right. A bronze bust of a siren from Olympia c. 700–600 BC. The figure once formed the handle of a bowl or cup.

The Greek Alphabet

A	B	Γ	Δ	E	Z	H	Θ	I	K	Λ	M
A	B	G	D	E	Z	E	Th	I	K	L	M

N	Ξ	O	Π	P	Σ	T	V	Φ	X	Ψ	Ω
N	X	O	P	R	S	T	U	Ph	Kh	Ps	O

The Greeks derived their alphabet from the Phoenician. We do not know, however, where and when the Greek alphabet came into existence. The earliest Greek inscriptions date from c. 750 BC, but the Greeks may have been writing earlier than that.

When the Greeks took over the Phoenician script, they adapted it and some changes in the pronunciation and form of the letters. For instance, they had to adapt some consonant signs and use them as vowel signs, as the Phoenician script did not employ signs for vowels.

Those who traded imported grain, timber, salted fish and luxury goods such as purple dye and papyrus. The Greeks exported wine, olive oil and pottery.

THE GREEKS SPREAD ABROAD The poet Hesiod, who lived in the late eighth century BC, described the hard work and difficult life of the farmers. One way to escape this life and get rich was to go to sea, and many Greeks did.

Much of Greece is mountainous and the soil is poor. In times of hardship, some left their homes and emigrated to places where larger areas of more fertile land were available. They went in groups and formed colonies in the new regions. You can see the large number of colonies that the Greeks established by looking at the map. In this way Greek influence spread throughout the Mediterranean.

By about 700 BC the towns were expanding. Because the many hills and mountains made transport and communication difficult, each town with its surrounding territory needed to be a self-sufficient, independent unit. As wealth increased and the towns grew they developed into city states.

CLASSICAL GREECE

The acropolis of Athens as it would have appeared during the Classical era. The building at the top was the Parthenon.

There were many city states with different traditions and forms of government. The Greek city state was called a 'polis' from which comes our word 'political.'

The two most powerful states were Athens and Sparta. Sparta, in particular was quite unlike other great states. Its customs were very severe and designed to produce soldiers; all male citizens had to be full-time soldiers.

Boys were taken from their mothers when they were seven and brought up together under very harsh conditions. They had no extra clothes in winter and were only fed porridge. The young men lived together and trained to be soldiers, hunted and supervised the serfs (called *helots*) who did all the work for them.

ATHENIAN DEMOCRACY Athens had a *democracy* which meant government by the people. All citizens had the right to attend a monthly 'assembly' and to vote on matters of the city. Only adult men who had been born in Athens were 'citizens,' and so women and slaves were not allowed to vote. So great was the power of the citizens or 'demos,' the people, that they could send a politician into exile, or *ostracize* him. This could happen if a minimum of 4000 citizens wrote the politician's name on an ostrakon which was a piece of broken pottery. There were no lawyers and people represented themselves in

court. To show the verdict, the jury used small discs for indicating 'guilty' or 'not guilty.'

THE PERSIAN WARS Athens' wealth came from the silver mine at Laureion and her natural harbor, the Peiraeus. The Athenians used some of the silver to build a fleet to protect themselves against Persian attack.

In 490 BC the Persian king Darius invaded Greece. The Persians, however, were quickly defeated at the battle of Marathon in 490 BC. The news was carried to Athens over 24 miles away by one runner. The race we know as the 'marathon' gets its name from this historical event. Ten years later, the Persians attacked again. At the battle of Thermopylae, their king and army was held up by only 300 Spartans. The Persians overcame this and advanced to Athens. At the naval battle of Salamis the Greek ships finally defeated the Persians.

After the Persian defeat, Athens became leader of an alliance set up against the prospect of another Persian attack. States contributed funds to be used to drive the Persians from the Greek cities of Asia Minor. The Athenians used this money to beautify their city. They built the Parthenon—the temple of Athena, the city goddess. This was on the top of the *acropolis*, meaning the 'high city,' where many other city buildings were situated.

The Athenian Democratic System

These pieces of broken pottery, or potsherds, were called 'ostraka.' When a total of 4000 Athenian citizens scratched the name of the same politician on these ostraka, that politician would be exiled from Athens— or 'ostracized.'

These metal discs were used as jurors' ballots in the law courts. If a juror was voting for the acquittal of a defendant, he would place a disc that had a solid hub into the ballot box. If voting for the condemnation of the defendant, a disc with a hollow hub was used.

The device above was a water clock which was used to mark the length of time a speaker might be allowed in the Assembly of the people. When the water had flowed from the higher pot into the lower pot, his time was up.

The Greek Achievement

The Greeks were great experimenters and innovators in many areas such as philosophy, architecture, literature, sculpture and politics. Their theories about science and medicine, though often wrong, were accepted by western Europe up until a few hundred years ago. Below are listed some of the key areas of Greek achievement.

Philosophy Socrates was an Athenian philosopher who devoted his life to enquiring into what the best way is for a person to conduct his/her life. Socrates himself did not write books, but his followers included Plato, another great philosopher in his own right, who recorded various of Socrates' philosophical dialogues.

Socrates was but one of a number of thinkers who have greatly influenced western thought. Other great philosophers of this period included Plato, Aristotle and Pythagoras.

Historians It was the Greeks who began the practice of recording history. Herodotus wrote his great work, the *Historia*, which was an account of the conflict between the Greeks and Persians

A mural from a Roman villa at Ephesus in Turkey depicting Socrates.

and how it had come to happen. Thucydides was an Athenian general who wrote an account of the Peloponnesian War between Athens and Sparta.

Dramatists Greek drama was rooted in the ritual festivities of various gods. By the fifth century BC various forms of drama had evolved, including tragedies, comedies and satyr plays. Competitions were held to assess the best work of drama, and writers such as Sophocles, Aeschylus and Euripides wrote tragedies that are still played and adapted today. The great comedic writer of this period was Aristophanes.

Sculpture The art of sculpture became increasingly naturalistic in this period. Just as the Greeks delighted in intellectual pursuit, so the human body was to be admired. The greatest sculptor of this period was Praxiteles.

A modern bronze statue of Leonidas, the Spartan king who died in 480 BC while defending the pass of Thermopylae against the Persians.

Key City States in Classical Greece

MACEDONIA

DELPHI •
• THEBES
CORINTH •
OLYMPIA •
• ATHENS
• ARGOS
SPARTA •

AEGEAN SEA

Area of Classical Greek civilization

The Greek civilization was small when compared with the empires of the Persians, Chinese and Indians. The area occupied by the city states of Classical Greece was not much larger than a Persian satrapy. Only a quarter of the land could be cultivated, and so ancient Greece never exceeded a population of 2,000,000.

THE RISE OF MACEDON

The Macedonian Army

Far left.
In the Macedonian phalanx, soldiers kept the enemy at bay by using their very long thrusting spears called 'sarissas.' This allowed the cavalry to charge at a weak spot in the enemy line, so breaking up the ranks.

Left.
Macedonian soldier wearing helmet, cuirass and greaves (leg armor), and carrying a spear and shield.

The Macedonian army was largely the product of the efforts of Philip II. As a young man in Thebes he had studied Greek military methods.

He decided that the best opposition to the Greek hoplites would be the phalanx. This was armed with a new weapon called the 'sarissa.' It was a pike twice as long as an ordinary spear.

These were carried by ranks of soldiers standing further apart than the hoplite soldiers. In this way, the sarissas of the men behind stuck forward between the soldiers in the front ranks. The effect was that of a cluster of sharp objects, like a hedgehog.

In addition there was an armored cavalry and a siege-train of heavy weapons, including catapults, to back up the phalanx. The Macedonian army was very formidable.

Left. Greek bronze helmet c. fifth century BC from Salonika.

As Athens became more powerful and exerted control over other Greek states, these states looked to Sparta for help. This led to the Peloponnesian War which lasted for 27 years until Sparta defeated Athens in 404 BC. During its course, the struggle raged over the whole of the Greek world. Thucydides, an Athenian historian, wrote an historical account to explain why it happened. As he pointed out, the war was prolonged and on an immense scale. All the states involved were exhausted at the end.

Sparta was now the ruling power amongst the Greeks. Sparta's political system was called *oligarchy* – the rule of the few over the many – and the Spartans despised democracy. Democrats were killed and in many other ways the Spartans abused their power. The other cities turned against them and in 371 BC Thebes rose up and defeated the Spartans. Soon afterwards the *helots* revolted successfully and Sparta's power was broken.

MACEDON BECOMES POWERFUL For a short while Thebes dominated Greece, but conflict soon broke out again which exhausted the Greek states. Their weakness now enabled King Philip of Macedon to take advantage of this situation and gain control of Greece.

Macedonia lay to the northeast of Greece and was very wealthy because it controlled a gold mine. The Greeks had always regarded Macedonia as a barbaric backwater, and were scornful of its claim to be Greek. It was on the fringes of Greece, and most people were hillsmen and shepherds until Philip's victories.

Macedonia was still a kingdom, a form of government long abandoned by Greeks. Many Greeks, particularly

Macedonian Wealth

Recent excavations at Vergina, where the Macedonian royal family were buried, have shown how wealthy they were. Splendid gold funeral wreaths, jewelry, diadems, a gold bow case or *gorytas* of Scythian style are among the objects found. There is a beautiful gold box or *larnax* containing human bones, thought to be those of Philip. A pair of *greaves* (worn to protect the front of the legs from knee to ankle – rather like hockey pads – only made of metal) is also thought to have belonged to him,

because one is longer than the other and Philip is known to have had a bad leg. There are also bronze and silver drinking vessels, and even fragments of silk cloth.

Above. Gold wreath from the Royal Tombs at Vergina. Such wreaths, of thin gold foil, were made as funerary wreaths.

Above. Iron Cuirass (breastplate) from the Royal Tombs at Vergina c. 350–325 BC. It is decorated with gold and features lion's heads which were a symbol of royalty. **Right. Gold larnax, or chest, containing human bones.** These are thought to be the bones of Philip of Macedon. It is from the Royal Tombs at Vergina.

Key Dates

359 BC	Accession of Philip II of Macedon.
356–355 BC	Philip defeats a coalition of northern barbarians; birth of Alexander.
352 BC	Philip victorious in Thessaly.
346 BC	Peace and alliance sworn to Philip and his descendants by Athens and her allies.
343–342 BC	Aristotle becomes Alexander's teacher.
338–337 BC	Philip enters Peloponnese; founds the peace and alliance of the League of Corinth.
336 BC	Murder of Philip. Alexander succeeds him.
334 BC	Alexander crosses to Asia. Battle of Granicus.
332–331 BC	Alexander in Egypt. Foundation of Alexandria.
327 BC	Invasion of India by Alexander.
323 BC	Alexander dies in Babylon.

Right. Ivory head of Philip II from the Royal Tombs at Verginia.

the Athenians, disliked kingship and were proud of their democracy.

KING PHILIP SPREADS MACEDONIAN INFLUENCE

Under Philip, Macedon had grown strong and expanded. A new weapon, a long spear, called the *sarissa,* had revolutionized the army's fighting tactics. Philip also had trained his army well and led them courageously in battle, even losing an eye in one battle.

Philip now began to buy support in the Greek states. In 338 BC he advanced to Chaeronaea in central Greece and defeated the Thebans and Athenians. He returned, victorious to Macedon only to be murdered in 336 BC. He had planned to fight against the Persians in Asia Minor to spread Macedonian influence even further, but this task was left to his son, Alexander, to carry out.

THE CONQUESTS OF ALEXANDER THE GREAT

On the death of Philip II of Macedon in 336 BC, his 20-year old son Alexander succeeded him. After making sure his kingship would not be taken away, he invaded Asia Minor in 334 BC. It is not certain whether Alexander planned to conquer the Persian Empire at the outset. But as time went by this certainly did become his aim.

The main part of his army consisted of 12,000 Macedonians and 12,000 Greeks. The troops were well trained and followed Alexander loyally. He was a brave and courageous commander and always led his men into battle. He narrowly escaped death on several occasions.

THE PERSIAN AND MACEDONIAN ARMIES The Persian King Darius III was an inexperienced military leader compared with Alexander who had fought under his father and had commanded troops even in his youth. The Persians took enormous baggage trains and even the royal ladies on their military campaigns. All the tents, furnishings and luxuries were a hindrance to swift movement.

By contrast, the Macedonian army was highly trained and efficient. The Macedonian *phalanx* was a formidable unit designed to break through the enemies ranks. It could also take up defensive positions when it was under attack. Pikes (the Macedonian *sarissa*, introduced by Philip) held by the front ranks formed the attack while behind, the soldiers held their shields up to deflect missiles.

THE CONQUEST OF PERSIA AND EGYPT Following Alexander's victory at Granicus, he moved along the west of Asia Minor taking cities such as Miletus which had withstood him. He wintered in Anatolia before reaching Issus (see map). Here he defeated a huge Persian army. After beseiging Tyre for several months, he took control of the city and then moved south to Egypt.

Alexander was welcomed in Egypt because the former Persian rulers had been harsh. He then turned north and east, winning his major victory at Gaugamela in northern Mesopotamia. Darius fled north to Bactria and was murdered by Bactrian nobles.

Persia and Egypt were now Alexander's, but still the conquests continued. The troops, however, were weary after fighting in the most distant region of northern Iran. Finally, in northern India, Alexander's army refused to go any further.

Now master of the Persian empire, Alexander attempted to unite the Greeks, Persians and Macedonians. He married Roxanne, the daughter of a Bactrian nobleman, and encouraged his soldiers to marry Persian women. Gradually he adopted Persian dress and behaved like an Eastern ruler, which his Macedonian and Greek troops did not like.

He was planning a campaign to Arabia, when he died in Babylon in 323. His son, born after his death, was killed by ambitious generals. Alexander's Empire was divided into kingdoms ruled by his former generals, to avoid any one getting too much power. These were called the 'Successors,' and for many years war raged across Greece and the Near East as they each established their control.

The Education of Alexander

From the age of seven, Alexander had been in the care of a strict tutor who had trained him in very Spartan ways. Very quickly he could ride well and had proved his prowess with Bucephalus, his beloved horse. He could also play the lyre and sing, and could recite Homer's *Iliad*.

An engraving depicting Plato who had been Aristotle's teacher.

When he was 13 years old, Aristotle, the great Athenian philosopher, became his teacher. Aristotle had studied under Plato, who in turn had studied under Socrates (see page 61). Aristotle's approach to philosophy was scientific, and he taught Alexander botany and zoology.

All his life,

A 12th century AD carving depicting Aristotle.

Alexander was to maintain an interest in science, and also in medicine. Alexander benefited from learning under Aristotle for four years, and the knowledge he gained helped him to become a great leader and military strategist.

The Empire of Alexander the Great

→ Route of Alexander's campaigns

■ Maximum extent of the Empire

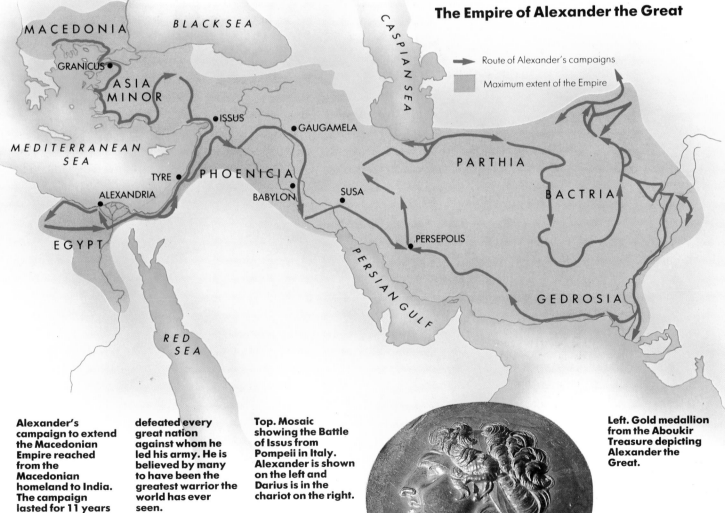

MACEDONIA

BLACK SEA

CASPIAN SEA

GRANICUS •

ASIA
MINOR

MEDITERRANEAN
SEA

ISSUS •

• GAUGAMELA

PARTHIA

TYRE •

PHOENICIA

BABYLON •

SUSA •

BACTRIA

ALEXANDRIA

EGYPT

PERSIAN GULF

PERSEPOLIS •

RED
SEA

GEDROSIA

Alexander's
campaign to extend
the Macedonian
Empire reached
from the
Macedonian
homeland to India.
The campaign
lasted for 11 years
and in that time he

defeated every
great nation
against whom he
led his army. He is
believed by many
to have been the
greatest warrior the
world has ever
seen.

Top. Mosaic
showing the Battle
of Issus from
Pompeii in Italy.
Alexander is shown
on the left and
Darius is in the
chariot on the right.

Left. Gold medallion
from the Aboukir
Treasure depicting
Alexander the
Great.

THE SPREAD OF GREEK INFLUENCE

The 300 years from Alexander's death to the start of Roman Empire are called the *Hellenistic Age*. This means 'Greek,' from *Hellas*, the name the Greeks gave to their country.

Because the eastern Mediterranean and parts of the Near East were ruled by Greek kings, there was naturally a strong Greek influence in that region.

Alexander's conquest took Greek soldiers as far as India. Along the way he founded towns in which some soldiers stayed behind, making new lives, and usually marrying local women. This was one way in which the east became *Hellenized*.

THE DISCOVERY OF AI KHANUM Some years ago, the King of Afghanistan was out hunting near the border with Russia. He noticed some Greek column fragments. French archaeologists excavated and found a completely Greek town. This town is called Ai Khanum, and you can see on the map how far it is from Greece. Here, in distant Bactria, Greeks visited the gymnasium to box and wrestle; they saw Greek plays and spoke the *koine*, the 'common language,' the most widely used language of the time and the one in which part of the Christian New Testament was written.

Ai Khanum was only a village compared with the new Greek cities nearer to the Mediterranean. The Greek rulers of Babylonia built a new capital, Seleucia, to replace the ancient city of Babylon.

ALEXANDRIA In Egypt, the ruling family – the Ptolemies – ruled from the new Greek city of Alexandria (named for Alexander the Great) on the Mediterranean. Here there were splendid harbors with ships bringing luxury goods from all over the known world. In the huge royal granary the grain of Egypt was stored.

The city had the most famous library of the ancient world, with 700,000 roles of papyrus. Scientists and mathematicians all worked here, including Euclid whose geometry was still taught in schools until recently. At the first museum in the world, the Mouseion, scholars were paid generously to carry out their research.

Life was less pleasant for manual workers in the gold mines. Working conditions were terrible and children worked alongside slaves.

For the wealthier members of the community, there were many ways of relaxing. On holidays they could visit the theater as well as attend processions with dancing

The Lighthouse at Alexandria

The great lighthouse was designed in the early Ptolemaic period and was dedicated by Sostratus of Cnidus in 279 BC. It was known as the 'Pharos' and was one of the Seven Wonders of the Ancient World.

No remains are left today of the lighthouse, though an approximate appearance can be reconstructed from various ancient accounts. It stood on a rock at the end of a causeway which divided the two large harbors of Alexandria. It was built with three stories and was 132 yards high. A fire burned permanently at the top, and was magnified and projected by a reflector so that it could be seen from a long distance. Horses were probably used to cart the fuelwood to the top, up a series of ramps.

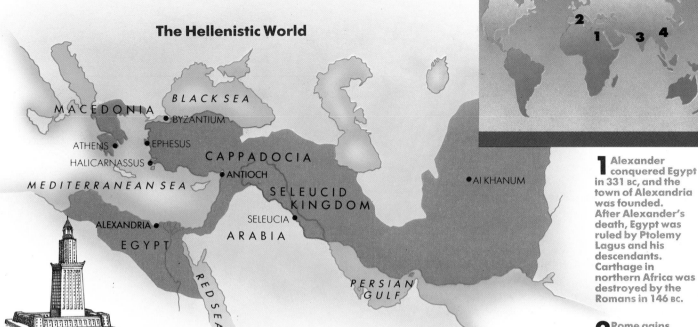

The Hellenistic World

The Hellenistic world covered a vast area. Archaeological remains showing Greek influence have been found as far away from Greece as Ai Khanum in present-day Afghanistan. The Pharos Lighthouse at Alexandria was one of the great architectural achievements of this period.

Left. Part of the frieze from the Great Altar of Zeus at Pergamon in Asia Minor. It depicts the fight between the gods and giants. It dates from c. 180–150 BC.

Below. A fine example of a Hellenistic statue of a boy athlete from Tralles. It dates from the third century BC.

1 Alexander conquered Egypt in 331 BC, and the town of Alexandria was founded. After Alexander's death, Egypt was ruled by Ptolemy Lagus and his descendants. Carthage in northern Africa was destroyed by the Romans in 146 BC.

2 Rome gains control of Italy c. 250 BC. Greek states are destroyed by the Romans in 146 BC and many Greek statues, paintings and books are plundered and taken back to Rome. Augustus becomes sole ruler of the Roman Empire in 27 BC.

3 In India, the Mauryan Empire is founded by Chandragupta in 322 BC. The first alphabetic Brahman script is used in India c. 250 BC.

4 China is unified under the Ch'in Dynasty in 221 BC. The building of the Great Wall of China commences. Around 100 BC, Indian religions begin to spread to China along trade routes.

and music. Games and chariot racing were held in the stadium, and men and boys exercised and met their friends at the gymnasium. Around the bustling market square were wine and food shops and stalls, selling everything from oil lamps to leather sandals and sweetmeats.

NEW LANDS At Pergamon in Asia Minor, beautiful gardens were created and sick people came to be healed at the sanctuary of Aesclepius.

The wealth of these new lands attracted Greeks from the homeland. In time the eastern Greeks learned non-Greek ways, and many changed their religion. They even worshiped the ruler as a *god king*, something which would have been unthinkable in the Classical Greek world.

AN INTERNATIONAL AGE In some ways this age was like ours: restless, urban, open to change and above all, *cosmopolitan*.

The Eastern World
ARYAN INDIA

Some time after 2000 BC people known as *Aryans* settled in northwest India. Gradually they moved east, until by 1000 BC, they had also settled in the upper valley of the Ganges River. Their language was an Indo-European one, an old form of *Sanskrit* which forms the basis of the north Indian languages spoken today.

Apart from language, some aspects of today's Indian culture, for instance the *caste system*, can be traced back to the Aryans. There are also Aryan elements in the *Hindu* religion such as certain gods. We know about Aryan gods and about the social structure of these people, from literature that was passed on orally until it was written down in about AD 1300.

The *Rig-Veda* is a collection of hymns. It portrays a picture of Aryans living in farming communities together with the original non-Aryan people, whom they dominated.

THE CASTE SYSTEM Early Aryan society was divided into four social groups. The first were the priests, called *Brahmans*. Next were the warriors or *Kshatriyas*. Third, the merchants, farmers and craftsmen, known as the *Vish*, and lastly the *Shudras* who were laborers and servants. Even lower, were the non-Aryans in India.

This social group system eventually developed into the caste system. Eventually there were hundreds of

Images of the Buddha in human form, as shown here, began to appear from the first century AD. The Buddha is generally shown meditating or preaching. Here the Buddha sits in the traditional cross-legged pose. The very act of making images of the Buddha was highly respected and valued. Wherever Buddhism spread, a great many images were sure to proliferate, and many of these images have survived to the present day. This image can be seen today at the Lahore Museum in Pakistan.

castes and sub-castes. The non-Aryans were regarded as 'unclean' and became the *outcasts* or *untouchables*. They did all the unpleasant work.

HOMES AND CITIES There are no remains of the homes of these Aryans, but we know from their poems that they lived in houses of wood and bamboo. These decay quickly leaving no archaeological evidence.

Large cities, the capitals of some 16 separate states, had been established in northern India by about 600 BC. Their names are known from two Sanskrit epics, the *Mahabharata* and the *Ramayana*. A number of such sites, one with a beautiful palace, have been excavated. As elsewhere, ironworking became widespread and the new tools increased food production. Other developments such as rice growing date from about 500 BC when people began to write and to use coinage.

THE SPREAD OF BUDDHISM In 563 BC the *Buddha* meaning 'the Enlightened one,' whose name was Siddhartha Gautama Buddha, was born in India. He lived the life of a rich nobleman until he was 29. Then he set out to try and understand what lay behind human existence. Gautama meditated and fasted and spent the rest of his life as a wandering preacher. He rejected the Brahmans' emphasis on rituals. The priestly class of Brahmans – who studied the sacred literature – performed all the sacrifices and rituals of the *Vedic* religion.

Gautama preached a very simple philosophy. *Nirvana*, or Enlightenment could be achieved by following a life of good conduct. The Buddha died in 483 BC and this religion spread through much of India and the eastern world.

INVADERS OF INDIA In 533 BC northwest India was invaded by the Persians. The site of the city of Taxila, now in Pakistan, dates from this time. Persian influence can be seen in some early Indian sculpture.

In 326 BC Alexander the Great reached the Punjab in northwest India. Here he fought against Poros. Although he did not stay long, Greek influence remained in the Indo-Greek cities of northwest India and Afghanistan. Shortly after Alexander's death, Chandragupta Maurya drove the Greeks out of the Punjab and founded the Mauryan *dynasty*, whose capital was at Pataliputra on the Ganges. These rulers united India.

The Spread of Buddhism

By the time the Buddha died, thousands of people in India had become his followers. This process was helped by the conversion of the Mauryan Emperor Asoka to Buddhism in the third century BC. Until Asoka died in

232 BC, India enjoyed a golden period of Buddhist rule. Hinduism was restored in India in about 183 BC, when an army general, named Pusyamitra Sunga, seized power from the last of the Mauryan emperors. The Kushan Empire, which extended from central Asia to northern India, reinstated Buddhism in India at the end of the first century AD. During the next centuries Buddhist teaching spread throughout most of Asia. It mingled with the traditional beliefs of many countries. Today there are well over 500 million Buddhists, mainly in such countries as India, Nepal, China, Japan, Korea, Tibet, Cambodia, Laos, Vietnam, Malaysia, Myanmar, Thailand and Sri Lanka.

1 States begin to arise in the Red Sea area, exporting frankincense and myrrh c. 550 BC. The first copper smelting begins in Niger and Mali c. 500 BC.

2 The Assyrian Empire comes to an end in 612 BC. The New Babylonian Empire emerges in 600 BC, and the rise of the Persian empire commences c. 550 BC. In 332 BC Alexander the Great begins his conquests and the Persian Empire falls.

3 480 BC marked the beginning of the Classical period in Greece. The Parthenon comes to completion on the Athenian acropolis.

4 Siddhartha Gautama, the Buddha, is born in northern India in 563 BC. Iron production begins in China c. 550 BC, and the first coinage appears in 500 BC. At about the same period, Taxila in northern India becomes an important city, and it develops its own style of art, called Gandhara.

5 Early hieroglyphic writing appears at Monte Albán and Oaxaca in Mexico c. 500 BC. The Chavín temple complexes are completed in Peru c. 400 BC.

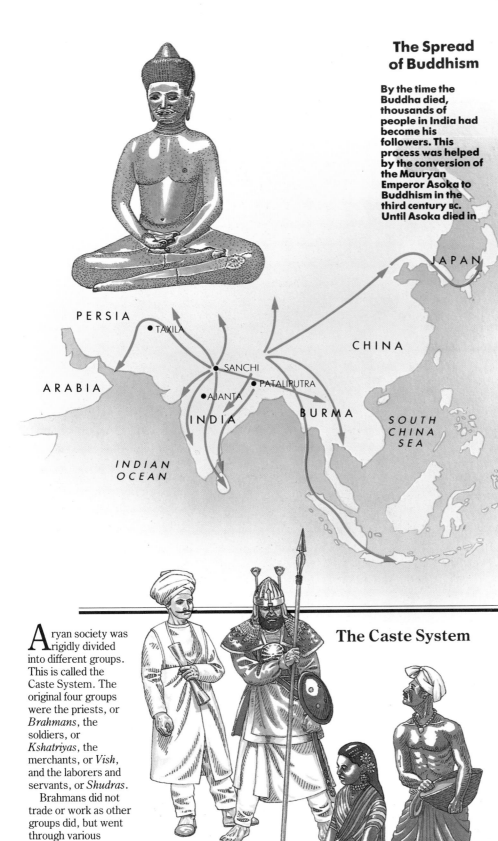

The Caste System

Aryan society was rigidly divided into different groups. This is called the Caste System. The original four groups were the priests, or *Brahmans*, the soldiers, or *Kshatriyas*, the merchants, or *Vish*, and the laborers and servants, or *Shudras*.

Brahmans did not trade or work as other groups did, but went through various stages of development to become completely pure and holy.

The Kshatriya is shown here in battle dress with a spear, sword and helmet. His weapons are made of iron.

The Vish worked in trade and were often, but not always, prosperous. Many of this caste in fact converted to other religions which did not divide society so rigidly.

The Shudras were the poorest and least educated group. If a Shudra cast his shadow on a member of another caste, that person would undergo various ritual purification and cleansing acts to rid themselves of 'pollution.'

These four figures each represent one of the groups of the caste system.

THE FIRST EMPIRES OF CHINA

Zhou China

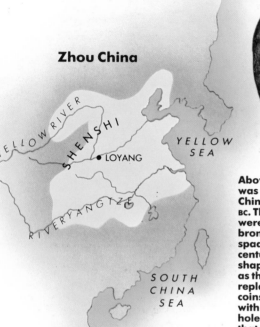

YELLOW RIVER
SHENSHI
• LOYANG
YELLOW SEA
RIVER YANGTZE
SOUTH CHINA SEA

Above. Coinage was first used in China around 500 BC. The earliest coins were miniature bronze knives and spades. By the third century simple disc-shaped coins such as this began to replace the earlier coins. Disc coins with a central hole in them, so that they could be threaded onto pieces of string, were to become the standard coin of the Han period.

Below. A statue showing Lao Tzu, an early Chinese philosopher, on his ox. He became very disappointed by events occurring within Zhou China, and so left his job and the country, traveling on an ox. As he was leaving, one of the officers on the border begged him to leave behind his teachings in writing. He agreed and wrote a book entitled *Tao Te Ching*, one of the central books of the Tao religion.

During the Zhou period, towns and cities were increasing in size and number. Buildings during this period were generally made of wood, so little survives except for the rammed earth foundations. The types of building found during the Zhou period progressed beyond those found in the Shang era, and ceremonial centers and industrial buildings began to spring up.

The dynasty of the *Zhou*, which overthrew the Shang rulers in about 1100 BC, lasted for nearly 1000 years. The first part of this period is called the Western Zhou as the capitals were in Shenshi (see map). From 771 BC to 481 BC was the Eastern Zhou period, the capital was near Loyang in Honan. The final phase is called the Warring States period which ended in 221 BC.

THE POWER OF FEUDAL ESTATES Although this 1000 years takes its name from the Zhou dynasty, their control of the whole country ended in the eighth century BC. The Western Zhou state was really a continuation of the Shang feudal-style government. The Zhou kings kept power by granting feudal estates to relatives and trustworthy nobles, who in turn gave them political and military allegiance. Gradually, the king lost his power as the feudal lords became stronger and combined against each other or against the king.

These lords had complete control over their territories. They grew wealthy from the profits of the salt and iron trades.

In the Eastern Zhou period there was a struggle for supremacy, which shifted from state to state. By the fifth century, the beginning of the Warring States period, no fewer than seven kingdoms had emerged.

NEW DEVELOPMENTS In spite of the unsettled political situation, the period from the eighth century was one of new developments and change. Iron technology was just one development, and from about 500 BC, the Chinese

Left. Confucius was China's most honored philosopher. His Chinese name was K'ung Ch'ui. During his lifetime he travelled from one noble's court to another telling them how people ought to behave. Most of the nobles would not listen to him. Later on, however, some of his disciples gained important positions and were able to put his teachings into practice.

Right. Ritual vessel of the Zhou Dynasty. It is made from bronze with a gold sheet overlay.

Chinese Writing

The chart below shows how Chinese characters developed from early picture signs to less recognizable symbols. Several thousand different pictures were used as words during the Zhou Dynasty.

	SUN	MOON	TREE	BIRD	HORSE
ABOUT 1500 BC					
BEFORE 213 BC					
AFTER AD 200	日	月	木	鳥	馬

were making enormous quantities of iron tools and weapons.

The new and better tools increased food production, as did improved forms of irrigation. In turn, the population grew, and so did the size and number of towns and cities. China became wealthier and coinage was introduced in this period.

The use of writing spread beyond oracle bones, which fell from use. In the large cities, official records and archives were kept. Writing was done either on strips of bamboo or on lengths of silk.

CONFUCIUS This was also a time when literature began to develop. In 551 BC Confucius was born. As a young man he began to teach his philosophy. His work of

Chinese history, *Spring and Autumn Annals*, was written shortly before he died in 479 BC. He claimed no original ideas, but believed that people could become good by the virtuous example of others – particularly those in positions of authority. Eventually his teachings became widely accepted.

LAO TZU Lao Tzu was another influential thinker. He believed that people should go back to leading a simple life, without any government interference, and in harmony with nature. He and his followers taught *Tao*, 'the way of nature,' as a way of life. Both thinkers were reacting to the confusion of their time, which culminated in the conquest of all the other states by the *Ch'in* ruler in 221 BC.

The Great Empires
TIME CHART

BC	NEAR EAST	AFRICA/EGYPT	EUROPE/GREECE	CHINA/INDIA
1150			Dorians invade Greece	
1140		First Phoenician colony in North Africa		
1027				Defeat of Shang Zhou Dynasty
1000>926	Israel's Monarchy			
900>750			Rise of city-states	
814		Phoenician city of Carthage founded		
745>630	Assyrian Empire			
700>600			Athenians expel kings	
700>500				Weakening of Zhou
625>539	Neo Babylonian Empire			
612	Nineveh sacked			
600				Early cities in Ganges valley
563				Birth of Buddha
551				Birth of Confucius
539	Cyrus conquers Babylon			
533				Achaemenid invasion of India
525>404		Egypt ruled by Persians		
507			Athenian democracy	
490>479			Persian Wars	
481>221				Warring States period – China
431>404			Peloponnesian War	
364>324				Nanda Dynasty – India
360	Weakening of Persia			
356>338			Philip in Greece	
343>332		Egypt's second period of Persian rule		
336>323			Alexander the Great	
334>323	Alexander the Great's campaigns			
334	Alexander invades Persian Empire			
332	Alexander conquers Mesopotamia	Alexander the Great invades Egypt		
	Alexander dies in Babylon			
326				Alexander in India
324>187				Mauryans drive out Greeks
304>64	Seleucids into Mesopotamia			
304>30		Ptolemaic period		
256>221				Ch'in unify empire
247>227	Parthian kingdom established			
232				Asoka's death
206				Collapse of Ch'in dynasty

GLOSSARY

acropolis   The highest part of an ancient Greek city, where the temples and other sacred structures were situated.

alloy   A mixture of metals, for example, bronze, which is a mixture of tin and copper. Alloys can occur naturally or be man-made.

alluvial   Fertile soil carried down-river and deposited on surrounding land by flooding.

alphabetic   A writing system in which each symbol represents a sound. First used by the Phoenicians and adopted by the Greeks.

archaeologist   One who studies the remains of antiquity and excavates to find evidence.

Aryans   A large group of people using Indo-European languages. The term is more usually used, however, to describe the Sanskrit-speaking invaders of India.

australopithecenes   The earliest known hominids to walk on two feet.

bandkeramik   Pottery decorated with incised linear designs and used by the earliest farming people of central Europe.

Brahmans   Priestly caste of the Aryans and of the Hindus in India.

Bronze Age   The period when bronze was used for tools and weapons. The actual time period varies from region to region; in the northeast it embraces the second millennium BC.

canopic jars   Egyptian funerary jars into which the organs of the dead person were placed.

caste system   Strict social order of classes or castes in India originating from the four main groups of Aryan society.

Ch'in   The dynasty from which China takes its name.

Chalcolithic   Stone Age period when copper was in use.

citadel   Raised fortress protecting a city or village.

cowrie shells   The shell of a sea mollusk used by various ancient and primitive peoples as jewelry, money or as magical objects.

crucible   Earthen pot for melting ores, metals, etc.

cuneiform   Wedge-shaped writing system effected with a reed stylus on clay tablets. It was invented by the Sumerians and used in the northeast for over 2000 years to express a number of languages.

cyclopean   Used to describe massive walls, as at Tiryns in Greece. It is derived from the word "Cyclopes," the one-eyed giants of Greek legend.

democracy   A government in which authority rests ultimately with the people, the *demos*.

dynasty   A succession of rulers of the same family.

epic poems   Long narrative poems relating heroic events in an elevated style.

gorytas   A quiver or bow-case of a particular style and used by the Scythians.

greaves   Armor covering the legs from knee to ankle.

Hapi   God of the River Nile (Egypt).

Hathor   Egyptian goddess of fertility and music. She is often shown with cow's ears.

Hellas   The Greeks' own name for their country.

Hellenistic Age   The term used to describe the period from the death of Alexander the Great until the rise of the Roman Empire.

helots   The name used for slaves in the town of Sparta in Greece.

hieroglyphic   Writing systems which use picture symbols.

Horus   Egyptian hawk god, son of Isis and Osiris.

Ice Age   Period when part of the earth was covered with ice and temperatures were much lower.

Iliad   Homeric epic relating the destruction of Troy by the Greeks.

Indo-European   A linguistic group relating to the language family that includes Sanskrit, Greek, Latin, Persian and most modern European languages.

irrigation   The provision of water for farming by means of canals.

Ishtar   The Mesopotamian goddess of love and war. The star was her symbol.

Isis   Egyptian goddess, wife of Osiris.

Ithaca   The Greek island where Odysseus' wife, Penelope, waited for him until he had completed the voyage of the *Odyssey*.

koine   The common Greek language spoken in the Hellenistic world.

Kshatriyas   The warrior caste of the Aryans.

labyrinth   The maze in which the minotaur is said to have lived at Knossos on the island of Crete.

larnax   Rectangular-shaped box or chest.

Linear A   Writing system used by the Minoans which has yet to be deciphered.

Linear B   Writing system found at Knossos on the island of Crete and at sites on the Greek mainland. It is an early form of Greek.

Longshan   Period in Chinese history which lasted from c. 2500–1800 BC.

Mahabharata   An Aryan/Hindu epic cycle which tells of a colossal war fought between two royal families.

megaliths   Monumental stone structures, for example, Stonehenge in England.

megaron   Large hall with a central hearth. This word was used in Mycenaean Greece.

Mesopotamia   Ancient term used to describe the land between the Tigris and Euphrates Rivers. This region is now found in modern Iraq.

Minoan The Bronze Age culture of Crete, named after King Minos.

minotaur The legendary animal, part-bull and part-man, that lived in the labyrinth of Knossos on the island of Crete.

monotheism Term used to describe a religion which worships only one god.

Mound People The Bronze Age people of Denmark.

mummy The dead body of an ancient Egyptian, bandaged and treated to endure for eternity.

natron A sulphur-like chemical used in ancient Egypt to dry out bodies before mummification.

Odyssey Homer's epic poem of the 10-year journey undertaken by the hero, Odysseus, after the fall of Troy.

oligarchy Government by the few over the many.

Osiris The Egyptian god of the dead.

papyrus Writing material made from the stem of the payrus plant, made by the Egyptians.

Pharaoh Title of the kings of ancient Egypt.

pictogram A picture used as a symbol in early forms of writing.

pithoi Large Greek ceramic storage jars.

Ptah The ancient Egyptian god of Memphis.

Ramayana An Aryan epic poem which tells the story of *Rama*, a dispossessed prince, and the abduction of his wife, Sita.

Re' Egyptian sun god.

Rig Veda An Aryan epic poem.

Sanskrit Language of the Aryans.

sarissa A long spear used by the Macedonians.

satrap A viceroy or governor of an ancient Persian province, or "satrapy."

Seth Egyptian god of destruction and the desert. He was the brother of Osiris.

shudras The lowest caste of the Aryans.

Spring and Autumn Annals The work of Confucius, the Chinese philosopher.

steppe A dry, grassy, generally treeless plain, as in the southeast of Europe and in Asia.

Stone Age The period when stone was used for tools and weapons.

transhumance The rearing of stock in two places: in the uplands in summer and in the lowlands in winter. It was practiced by some nomads.

ziggurat Temple towers built in Mesopotamia. The god's sanctuary was built at the very top.

INDEX

Further Reading

GENERAL REFERENCE
*Illustrated Atlas of World
    History* by Simon Adams,
    John Briquebec and Ann
    Kramer (Random House,
    1992)
Prehistory by Keith Branigan
    (Watts, Franklin, 1986)
*The Story of Mankind: the
    Classic History of All Ages
    for All Ages* by Hendrik W.
    Van Loon (Liveright, 1985)
How People First Lived by
    William Jaspersohn (Watts,
    Franklin, 1985)
*The Ancient World: 3,000
    B.C. – A.D. 476* by John
    Briquebec (Watts,
    Franklin, 1990)
The First Civilizations by
    Giovanni Caselli (Bedrick,
    Peter, 1985)

THE NEAR EAST AND
    MESOPOTAMIA
*The Earliest Civilizations:
    Ancient Greece and the
    Near East, 3,000 – 200
    B.C.* by Carol G. Thomas
    (University Press of
    America, 1982)

EGYPT

What Do We Know About the Egyptians? by Joanna Defrates (Bedrick, Peter, 1992)

The Egyptian World by Margaret Oliphant (Watts, Franklin, 1989)

An Egyptian Town by R. J. Unstead (Watts, Franklin, 1986)

Egypt by Anne Millard (Watts, Franklin, 1988)

Pyramids by Anne Millard (Watts, Franklin, 1989)

GREECE

Greece and the Persians by John S. Smith (Focus, 1989)

The Greeks by Anne Millard (E D C, 1990)

The Greeks by H. D. Kitto (Smith, Peter, 1988)

The Greek World by Anton Powell (Watts, Franklin, 1987)

Picture Acknowledgments

The author and publishers would like to acknowledge, with thanks,
the following photographic sources:
Front cover (left) C.M. Dixon, (right) Ancient Art & Architecture Collection; p, 13 AKG;
p. 18 (upper) Trustees of the British Museum; p. 19 Trustees of the British Museum;
p. 21 Michael Holford; p 23 (upper) C.M. Dixon, (center & lower) Trustees of the British
Museum; p. 24 (upper) Robert Harding Picture Library, (lower) Trustees of the British Museum;
p. 25 C.M. Dixon; p. 26 AKG; p. 27 (left) C.M. Dixon; p. 29 (upper) Michael Holford, (lower left)
Michael Holford, (lower center) Douglas Dickins, (lower right) Michael Holford; p. 30 (left) AKG,
(center) Robert Harding, (right) AKG; p. 32 C.M. Dixon; p. 33 (left) C.M. Dixon, (right) Sonia
Halliday Photographs; p. 34 AKG; p. 35 (left) Sonia Halliday Photographs, (right) Robert Harding
Picture Library; p. 36 (left & right) MacQuitty Collection; p. 39 (upper) C.M. Dixon, (center left)
C.M. Dixon, (center right) Ancient Art & Architecture Collection, (lower) Robert Harding
Picture Library; p. 43 (left & right) Ancient Art & Architecture Collection; p. 45 (upper left)
Ancient Art & Architecture Collection; (center) Michael Holford, (upper right) Michael Holford,
(lower right) Michael Holford; p. 47 (left & right) Werner Forman Archive; p. 49 (upper left &
right) Michael Holford, (center) Sonia Halliday Photographs, (lower) Werner Forman Archive;
p.50 Werner Forman Archive; p. 51 AKG; p. 52 (upper) M. Oliphant, (lower left & right)
Trustees of the British Museum; p. 53 (left) Mansell Collection, (right) Robert Harding
Picture Library; p. 54 MacQuitty Collection; p. 55 (upper & lower) Douglas Dickins;
p. 56 C.M. Dixon; p. 57 (upper, center, left & lower) Trustees of the British Museum,
(center right) Werner Forman Archive; p. 59 (upper & lower left) Michael Holford,
(lower right) Olympia Museum; p. 61 (upper) Sonia Halliday Photographs,
(lower) C.M. Dixon; p. 62 Michael Holford; p. 63 (all photographs) Ministry of Culture,
Archaeological Receipts Fund, Thessalonika Museum; p. 64 (upper & lower)
Mansell Collection; p. 67 (upper) M. Oliphant, (lower) Sonia Halliday Photographs;
p. 68 Macquitty Collection; p. 70 (upper & lower) Ancient Art & Architecture Collection;
p. 71 (left) The Bridgeman Art Library, (right) Werner Forman Archive.